Geotechnical Engineering
(Theory and Practice)

AUTHOR

Dr. Neelima Satyam
Professor,
Indian Institute of Technology, Indore,
Indore (M.P.), India

REVIEWER

Dr. P Shivananda
Professor,
REVA University,
Bangalore, India

KHANNA BOOK PUBLISHING CO. (P) Ltd.
4C/4344, Ansari Road, Darya Ganj,
New Delhi, India

All India Council for Technical Education
Nelson Mandela Marg, Vasant Kunj,
New Delhi, India

Dear Readers,

To prevent the piracy, this book is secured with HIGH SECURITY HOLOGRAM on the front title cover. In case you don't find the hologram on the front cover title, please write us to at contact@khannabooks.com or whatsapp us at +91-99109 09320 and avail special gift voucher for yourself.

Specimen of Hologram on front Cover title:

Moreover, there is a SPECIAL DISCOUNT COUPON for you with EVERY HOLOGRAM.

How to avail this SPECIAL DISCOUNT:

Step 1: Scratch the hologram

Step 2: Under the scratch area, your "coupon code" is available

Step 3: Logon to www.khannabooks.com

Step 4: Use your "coupon code" in the shopping cart and get your copy at a special discount

Step 5: Enjoy your reading!

ISBN: 978-93-5538-960-2
Book Code: DIP440EN

Geotechnical Engineering (Theory & Practicals)

by Dr. Neelima Satyam

First Edition: 2025

Originally Published by:
All India Council for Technical Education, Ministry of Education, GOI

Exclusively Published & Distributed by:
Khanna Book Publishing Co. (P) Ltd.
4C/4344, Ansari Road, Daryaganj,
New Delhi (INDIA)

Visit us at: **www.khannabooks.com**
Write us at: **contact@khannabooks.com**

To view complete list of books, Please scan the QR Code: KPH

Printed in Bharat.

प्रो. टी. जी. सीताराम
अध्यक्ष
Prof. T. G. Sitharam
Chairman

सत्यमेव जयते

आज़ादी का अमृत महोत्सव

अखिल भारतीय तकनीकी शिक्षा परिषद्
(भारत सरकार का एक सांविधिक निकाय)
(शिक्षा मंत्रालय, भारत सरकार)
नेल्सन मंडेला मार्ग, वसंत कुंज, नई दिल्ली–110070
दूरभाष : 011–26131498
ई–मेल : chairman@aicte-india.org

ALL INDIA COUNCIL FOR TECHNICAL EDUCATION
(A STATUTORY BODY OF THE GOVT. OF INDIA)
(Ministry of Education, Govt. of India)
Nelson Mandela Marg, Vasant Kunj, New Delhi-110070
Phone : 011-26131498
E-mail : chairman@aicte-india.org

FOREWORD

Engineers are the backbone of any modern society. They are the ones responsible for the marvels as well as the improved quality of life across the world. Engineers have driven humanity towards greater heights in a more evolved and unprecedented manner.

The All India Council for Technical Education (AICTE), have spared no efforts towards the strengthening of the technical education in the country. AICTE is always committed towards promoting quality Technical Education to make India a modern developed nation emphasizing on the overall welfare of mankind.

An array of initiatives has been taken by AICTE in last decade which have been accelerated now by the National Education Policy (NEP) 2020. The implementation of NEP under the visionary leadership of Hon'ble Prime Minister of India envisages the provision for education in regional languages to all, thereby ensuring that every graduate becomes competent enough and is in a position to contribute towards the national growth and development through innovation & entrepreneurship.

One of the spheres where AICTE had been relentlessly working since past couple of years is providing high quality original technical contents at Under Graduate & Diploma level prepared and translated by eminent educators in various Indian languages to its aspirants. For students pursuing 2nd year of their Engineering education, AICTE has identified 87 books, which shall be translated into 12 Indian languages - Hindi, Tamil, Gujarati, Odia, Bengali, Kannada, Urdu, Punjabi, Telugu, Marathi, Assamese & Malayalam. In addition to the English medium, books in different Indian Languages are going to support the students to understand the concepts in their respective mother tongue.

On behalf of AICTE, I express sincere gratitude to all distinguished authors, reviewers and translators from the renowned institutions of high repute for their admirable contribution in a record span of time.

AICTE is confident that these outcomes based original contents shall help aspirants to master the subject with comprehension and greater ease.

(Prof. T. G. Sitharam)

ACKNOWLEDGEMENT

The authors are grateful to the authorities of AICTE, particularly Prof. T. G. Sitharam, Chairman; Prof. M. P. Poonia, Vice-Chairman; Prof. Rajive Kumar, Member- Secretary and Dr Amit Kumar Srivastava, Director, Faculty Development Cell for their planning to publish the books on Geotechnical Engineering (Theory & Practicals). We sincerely acknowledge the valuable contributions of the reviewer of the book, Dr. P Shivananda, Professor, REVA University, Bangalore for his suggestions throughout the writing process.

This book is an outcome of various suggestions of AICTE members, experts and authors who shared their opinion and thought to further develop the engineering education in our country. Acknowledgements are due to the contributors and different workers in this field whose published books, review articles, papers, photographs, footnotes, references and other valuable information enriched us at the time of writing the book.

Dr. Neelima Satyam

PREFACE

The book titled "*Geotechnical Engineering (Theory & Practicals)*" is an outcome of the long experience of my teaching journey. The book aims to provide basic knowledge of Geotechnical engineering to diploma students. Keeping in mind the purpose of wide coverage as well as to provide essential supplementary information, we have included the topics recommended by AICTE, in a very systematic and orderly manner throughout the book. Efforts have been made to explain the fundamental concepts of the subject in the simplest possible way.

During the process of preparation of this book, we have considered the various standard textbooks and accordingly we have developed sections like critical questions, solved and supplementary problems etc. While preparing the different sections emphasis has also been laid on definitions and laws and on comprehensive synopsis of formulae for a quick revision of the basic principles. The book covers simple and medium level problems, and these have been presented in a very logical and systematic manner.

The book consists of illustrations, examples and exercises for each topic, along with simple descriptions. The book has five units as per AICTE guidelines, explaining the engineering behaviour of soil. It is important to note that in all the relevant units, we have included the concerned laboratory practical. In addition, besides some interesting information for the users under the heading "Know More" section after each unit. Dynamic QR codes are also used for further learning videos for interested students.

"Geotechnical Engineering (Theory & Practicals)" is meant to provide a thorough grounding in Geotechnical Engineering on the topics covered. This book will prepare engineering students to apply the knowledge of soil mechanics to tackle the engineering challenges and address the related aroused questions. The subject matters are presented in a constructive manner so that a diploma prepares students to work in construction industry or in national laboratories at the very forefront of technology.

We sincerely hope that the book will inspire the students to learn and discuss the ideas behind basic principles of geotechnical engineering and will surely contribute to the development of a solid foundation of the subject. We would be thankful to all beneficial comments and suggestions which will contribute to the improvement of the future editions of the book. It gives us immense pleasure to place this book in the hands of the teachers and students. It was indeed a big pleasure to work on different aspects covering in the book.

Dr. Neelima Satyam

OUTCOME BASED EDUCATION

For the implementation of an outcome based education the first requirement is to develop an outcome based curriculum and incorporate an outcome based assessment in the education system. By going through outcome based assessments, evaluators will be able to evaluate whether the students have achieved the outlined standard, specific and measurable outcomes. With the proper incorporation of outcome based education there will be a definite commitment to achieve a minimum standard for all learners without giving up at any level. At the end of the programme running with the aid of outcome based education, a student will be able to arrive at the following outcomes:

Programme Outcomes (POs) are statements that describe what students are expected to know and be able to do upon graduating from the program. These relate to the skills, knowledge, analytical ability, attitude and behaviour that students acquire through the program. The POs essentially indicate what the students can do from subject-wise knowledge acquired by them during the program. As such, POs define the professional profile of an engineering diploma graduate.

National Board of Accreditation (NBA) has defined the following seven POs for an Engineering diploma graduate:

PO-1. Basic and Discipline specific knowledge: Apply knowledge of basic mathematics, science and engineering fundamentals and engineering specialization to solve the engineering problems.

PO-2. Problem analysis: Identify and analyses well-defined engineering problems using codified standard methods.

PO-3. Design/development of solutions: Design solutions for well-defined technical problems and assist with the design of systems components or processes to meet specified needs.

PO-4. Engineering Tools, Experimentation and Testing: Apply modern engineering tools and appropriate technique to conduct standard tests and measurements.

PO-5. Engineering practices for society, sustainability and environment: Apply appropriate technology in context of society, sustainability, environment and ethical practices.

PO-6. Project Management: Use engineering management principles individually, as a team member or a leader to manage projects and effectively communicate about well-defined engineering activities.

PO-7. Life-long learning: Ability to analyse individual needs and engage in updating in the context of technological changes.

COURSE OUTCOMES

By the end of the course the students are expected to learn:

CO-1: Identify types of rocks and sub soil strata of earth.

CO-2: Interpret the physical properties of soil related to given construction activities.

CO-3: Use the results of permeability and shear strength test for foundation analysis.

CO-4: Interpret the soil bearing capacity results.

CO-5: Compute optimum moisture content values for maximum dry density of soil through various tests.

Mapping of Course Outcomes with Programme Outcomes to be done according to the matrix given below:

Course Outcomes	EXPECTED MAPPING WITH PROGRAMME OUTCOMES (1- Weak Correlation; 2- Medium correlation; 3- Strong Correlation)						
	PO-1	PO-2	PO-3	PO-4	PO-5	PO-6	PO-7
CO-1	3	2	1	1	1	1	3
CO-2	3	3	2	3	1	1	3
CO-3	3	3	2	3	1	1	3
CO-4	3	3	2	3	1	1	3
CO-5	3	3	2	3	1	1	3

GUIDELINES FOR TEACHERS

To implement Outcome Based Education (OBE) knowledge level and skill set of the students should be enhanced. Teachers should take a major responsibility for the proper implementation of OBE. Some of the responsibilities (not limited to) for the teachers in OBE system may be as follows:

- Within reasonable constraint, they should manoeuvre time to the best advantage of all students.
- They should assess the students only upon certain defined criterion without considering any other potential ineligibility to discriminate them.
- They should try to grow the learning abilities of the students to a certain level before they leave the institute.
- They should try to ensure that all the students are equipped with the quality knowledge as well as competence after they finish their education.
- They should always encourage the students to develop their ultimate performance capabilities.
- They should facilitate and encourage group work and team work to consolidate newer approach.
- They should follow Blooms taxonomy in every part of the assessment.

Bloom's Taxonomy

Level	Teacher should Check	Student should be able to	Possible Mode of Assessment
Creating	Students ability to create	Design or Create	Mini project
Evaluating	Students ability to Justify	Argue or Defend	Assignment
Analysing	Students ability to distinguish	Differentiate or Distinguish	Project/Lab Methodology
Applying	Students ability to use information	Operate or Demonstrate	Technical Presentation/ Demonstration
Understanding	Students ability to explain the ideas	Explain or Classify	Presentation/Seminar
Remembering	Students ability to recall (or remember)	Define or Recall	Quiz

GUIDELINES FOR STUDENTS

Students should take equal responsibility for implementing the OBE. Some of the responsibilities (not limited to) for the students in OBE system are as follows:

- Students should be well aware of each UO before the start of a unit in each and every course.
- Students should be well aware of each CO before the start of the course.
- Students should be well aware of each PO before the start of the programme.
- Students should think critically and reasonably with proper reflection and action.
- Learning of the students should be connected and integrated with practical and real life consequences.
- Students should be well aware of their competency at every level of OBE.

ABBREVIATIONS AND SYMBOLS

List of Abbreviations

General Terms			
Abbreviations	**Full form**	**Abbreviations**	**Full form**
CBR	California Bearing Ratio	OMC	Optimum Moisture Content
CD	Consolidated-Drained	RCC	Reinforced Cement Concrete
CU	Consolidated-Undrained	SPT	Standard Penetration Test
IS	Indian Standard	UU	Unconsolidated-Undrained
MDD	Maximum Dry Density		

List of Symbols

Symbols	Description	Symbols	Description
V_a	Volume of air voids	w_l	Liquid limit
a_c	Air content	w_p	Plastic limit
n_a	Percent air voids	w_s	Shrinkage limit
S	Degree of saturation	I_P	Plasticity index
e	Void ratio	I_s	Shrinkage index
V_W	Volume of water	I_l	Liquidity index
n	Porosity	I_c	Consistency index
V_v	Volume of voids	I_f	Flow index
V_S	Volume of solids	I_t	Toughness index
V	Total volume of soils	S_t	Sensitivity
w	Water content	k	Coefficient of permeability
W_w	Weight of water	v	Velocity
W_s	Weight of solids	i	Hydraulic gradient
W	Total weight of soil	t	Time
γ	Bulk unit weight	N_f	Number of flow channels
γ_d	Dry unit weight	N_d	Number of equipotential drops
γ_{sat}	Saturated unit weight	p_s	Seepage pressure
γ_{sub}	Submerged unit weight	τ_f	Shear strength of soil
γ_w	Unit weight of water	c	Cohesion of soil

Symbols	Description	Symbols	Description
G_m	Mass or bult specific gravity	σ	Normal stress on soil
G	True or absolute specific gravity	u	Pore water pressure
Cu	Uniformity coefficient	φ	Angle of internal friction
Cc	Coefficient of curvature	D_f	Depth of foundation
Dr or I_D	Relative density	K_o	Coefficient of earth pressure at rest
K_a	Coefficient of active earth pressure	K_p	Coefficient of passive earth pressure

LIST OF FIGURES

1. Overview of Geology and Geotechnical Engineering.......... 1

Fig. 1.1: Examples of igneous rocks 4
Fig. 1.2: Examples of sedimentary rocks 5
Fig. 1.3: Examples of sedimentary rocks 6
Fig. 1.4: Classification of transported soils 7
Fig. 1.5: (a) Shallow and (b) deep foundations 8
Fig. 1.6: Layers of pavement 9
Fig. 1.7: Retaining wall 9
Fig. 1.8: (a) Homogenous earthen dam, (b) Zoned earthen dam and (c) Diaphragm-type earthen dam 10

2. Physical and Index Properties of Soil.......... 13

Fig. 2.1: Phase diagrams of soil in the dry state, partially saturated state, and fully saturated state 14
Fig. 2.2: Three-phase diagram 14
Fig. 2.3: Particle size distribution curves 19
Fig. 2.4: Atterberg limits 20
Fig. 2.5: Flow curve 22
Fig. 2.6: Flow chart for classification of coarse-grained soils 23
Fig. 2.7: Plasticity chart and IS soil classification. 24
Fig. 2.8: Flow chart for classification of fine-grained soils 24

3. Permeability and Shear Strength of Soil.......... 40

Fig. 3.1: Constant permeability test 43
Fig. 3.2: Flow parallel to bedding planes 44
Fig. 3.3: Falling head permeability test 44
Fig. 3.4: Flow perpendicular to bedding planes 45
Fig. 3.5: Flow nets. (a) below a sheet pile, and (b) below a gravity dam 46
Fig. 3.6: Phreatic line through an earthen dam 49
Fig. 3.7: Phreatic line through an earthen dam with horizontal filter 50
Fig. 3.8: Piping through dam body and foundation 50
Fig. 3.9: Measures to control piping 51
Fig. 3.10: Failure envelopes for different types of soil 52
Fig. 3.11: Direct shear test (a) Failure envelope and (b) laboratory test set up 53
Fig. 3.12: Laboratory vane shear test setup 54

4. Bearing Capacity of Soil.......... 63

Fig. 4.1: Types of shear failure 66
Fig. 4.2: Depth of water table below foundation (a) Case 1 and (b) Case II 67
Fig. 4.3: Typical setup for plate load test 70

Fig. 4.4: Load intensity vs settlement for plate load test 70
Fig. 4.5: Relationship between lateral earth pressure and wall movement 73
Fig. 4.6: Earth pressure at rest 73
Fig. 4.7: Distribution of lateral earth pressure. (a) dry condition, (b) water table above the bottom of the wall and (c) water table at the top of backfill 74
Fig. 4.8: Active earth pressure 75
Fig. 4.9: Mohrs circle for active earth pressure condition 76
Fig. 4.10: Passive earth pressure 77
Fig. 4.11: Mohrs circle for passive earth pressure condition 77

5. Compaction and Stabilization of Soil 83
Fig. 5.1: Set up for light compaction as per IS 2720 (Part VII) 84
Fig. 5.2: Set up for heavy compaction as per IS 2720 (Part VIII) 85
Fig. 5.3: Compaction curve 86
Fig. 5.4: Compaction curves for light compaction and heavy compaction 87
Fig. 5.5: Compaction curve for cohesionless soils 88
Fig. 5.6: Different types of rollers 90
Fig. 5.7: Load penetration curves for CBR 93

LIST OF TABLES

2. Physical and Index Properties of Soil **13**
Table 2.1: Inter-relationships 18
Table 2.2: Consistency classification 21

4. Bearing Capacity of Soil **63**
Table 4.1: Terzaghi's bearing capacity factors 65
Table 4.2: Maximum and differential settlements (IS 1904 -1986) 69
Table 4.3: Correlation between N and φ 72

5. Compaction and Stabilization of Soil **83**
Table 5.1: Comparison between different compaction tests 85
Table 5.2: Some important properties and its side of optimum 87
Table 5.3: Difference between compaction and consolidation 90
Table 5.4: Penetration vs standard load for CBR 93
Table 5.5: Spacing of Borings (Sowers and Sowers, 1970) 96
Table 5.6: Depth of exploration (IS: 1892-1979) 96

CONTENTS

Foreword iii
Acknowledgement v
Preface vii
Outcome Based Education ix
Course Outcomes x
Guidelines for Teachers xi
Guidelines for Students xii
Abbreviations and Symbols xiii
List of Figures xv
List of Tables xvii

1. Overview of Geology and Geotechnical Engineering..1-12
Unit Specifics 1
Rationale 1
Pre-requisites 1
Unit Outcomes 1
1.1 Geology 2
1.1.1 Branches of Geology 2
1.1.1.1 Physical Geology 2
1.1.1.2 Petrology 2
1.1.1.3 Mineralogy 2
1.1.1.4 Structural Geology 2
1.1.1.5 Stratigraphy 2
1.1.1.6 Palaeontology 3
1.1.1.7 Economic Geology 3
1.1.1.8 Engineering Geology 3
1.1.2 Importance of Geology in Civil Engineering 3
1.2 Rocks 3
1.2.1 Igneous Rocks 4
1.2.2 Sedimentary Rocks 5
1.2.3 Metamorphic Rocks 6
1.3 Soil 7
1.3.1 Field Applications 8
1.3.1.1 Foundations 8
1.3.1.2 Pavements 8
1.3.1.3 Retaining structures 9
1.3.1.4 Earthen dam 9
Unit Summary 10
Exercises 10

Practicals 11
Know More 12
References and Suggested Readings 12

2. Physical and Index Properties of Soil....13-39

Unit Specifics 13
Rationale 13
Pre-requisites 13
Unit Outcomes 13
2.1 Soil as a Three-Phase System 14
2.1.1 Three Phase Diagrams 14
2.1.1.1 Void Ratio (e) 15
2.1.1.2 Porosity (n) 15
2.1.1.3 Degree of Saturation (S) 15
2.1.1.4 Percent Air Voids (n_a) 15
2.1.1.5 Air Content (a_c) 15
2.1.2 Water Content 15
2.1.3 Unit Weight of Soil 16
2.1.3.1 Bulk Unit Weight (γ) 16
2.1.3.2 Dry Unit Weight (γ_d) 16
2.1.3.3 Saturated Unit Weight (γ_{sat}) 16
2.1.3.4 Submerged Unit Weight (γ_{sub}) 16
2.1.3.5 Unit Weight of Soil Solids 17
2.1.4 Specific Gravity 17
2.1.4.1 Mass or Bulk specific Gravity (G_m) 17
2.1.4.2 True or Absolute Specific Gravity or Specific Gravity of Soil Solids (G) 17
2.1.5 Inter Relationships 18
2.2 Particle Size Distribution 18
2.2.1 Laboratory Analysis 18
2.2.2 Particle Size Distribution Curve 19
2.2.3 Relative Density 20
2.3 Consistency of Soil 20
2.3.1 Atterberg Limits 20
2.3.1.1 Liquid limit (w_l) 20
2.3.1.2 Plastic Limit (w_p) 21
2.3.1.3 Shrinkage Limit (w_s) 21
2.3.1.4 Plasticity Index (I_P) 21
2.3.1.5 Shrinkage Index (I_s) 21
2.3.1.6 Liquidity index (I_l) 21
2.3.1.7 Consistency Index (I_c) 21
2.3.1.8 Flow Index (I_f) 22

2.3.1.9 Toughness Index (I_t) 22
2.3.1.10 Sensitivity 22
2.3.1.11 Activity 22
2.3.1.12 Thixotropy 22
2.4 Classification of Soils – IS Classification System 23
Unit Summary 25
Exercises 25
Practicals 27
Know More 39
References and Suggested Readings 39

3. Permeability and Shear Strength of Soil 40-62
Unit Specifics 40
Rationale 40
Pre-requisites 40
Unit Outcomes 40
3.1 Permeability of Soil 41
3.1.1 Darcy's Law of Permeability 41
3.1.2 Coefficient of Permeability 42
3.1.3 Determination of Coefficient of Permeability 42
3.1.3.1 Constant Head Permeability Test 43
3.1.3.2 Falling Head Permeability Test or Variable Head Permeability Test 43
3.1.3.3 Field Tests 44
3.1.4 Permeability of Stratified Deposits 44
3.1.4.1 Average Permeability Parallel to Bedding Planes 44
3.1.4.2 Average Permeability Perpendicular to Bedding Planes 45
3.1.5 Seepage Analysis 45
3.1.5.1 Properties of Flow Net 46
3.1.5.2 Applications or Uses of Flow Net 47
3.1.6 Seepage Pressure 48
3.1.7 Concept of Effective Stress 48
3.1.7.1 Effective Stress 48
3.1.7.2 Pore Water Pressure 48
3.1.8 Seepage Velocity 49
3.1.9 Seepage Through Earthen Structures 49
3.1.9.1 Piping 50
3.2 Shear Strength of Soil 51
3.2.1 Components of Shearing Resistance 51
3.2.2 Classification of Soils 51
3.2.3 Mohr-Coulomb Failure Theory 52
3.2.4 Modified Mohr-Coulomb Failure Theory 52

AICTE'S LIST OF PRESCRIBED TEXTBOOKS

As Per Model Curriculum & Outcome Based Education

aligned with

NATIONAL EDUCATION POLICY 2020

UNDERGRADUATE COURSE BOOKS

S.No.	ISBN	Book Name	Author
1	9789355382160	Advanced Electrical Machines: Theory and Practicals	Bharat Singh Rajpurohit
2	9789355382139	Analog Electronic Circuits: Theory and Practical	Venu Sonti, Sachin Jain
3	9789355383808	Analog Electronic Devices: Theory and Practicals	N. B Balamurugan
4	9789391505158	Basic Electrical Engineering (with Lab Manual)	S.K. Sahdev
5	9789355388087	Basic of Electronics	Brijesh Iyer
6	9789355387127	Basics of Electrical Machines: Theory and Practicals	D. K. Palwalia, U. K. Kalla, R. K. Kumawat
7	9789355389381	Basics of Mechanics	Shubhankar Bhowmick, N. Venkata Swamy Naidu
8	9789355386250	Basics of Thermodynamics	Parmod Kumar, Atul Dhar
9	9789355386984	Biology for Engineers	Annamma Odaneth
10	9789391505141	Chemistry-I	Manisha Agarwal
11	9789355384843	Civil Engineering Societal and Global Impact	Shakuntala Acharya
12	9789355382184	Computer Aided Civil Engineering Drawing	D. Chandra Mouli, B. Swathi
13	9789355382580	Computer Aided Design & Analysis	Hari Kumar Voruganti
14	9789355387592	Computer Architecture	D. Vaithiyanathan
15	9789355385093	Computer Networks	Hari Prabhat Gupta
16	9789355385307	Construction Engineering & Management	Sparsh Johari
17	9789355388728	Control Systems	S.N. Deepa
18	9789355385420	Data Structure and Algorithms	Ranbir Singh Sanasam
19	9789355386700	Design and Analysis of Algorithms	Hari P. Gupta, Rahul Mishra
20	9789355388872	Digital Electronics and System	Abhishek Bhatt
21	9789355386571	Digital Signal Processing	Sanjeev Sharma
22	9789355383396	Disaster management	Pradeep K. Goyal, Anil K. Gupta
23	9789355385222	Discrete Mathematical Structures	Narendra S. Chaudhari, Sharmila S. P.
24	9789355387868	Effective Technical Communication	Pritee Sharma, Sanchita Verma
25	9789355383389	Electrical Circuit Analysis and Network Theory	Shouri Chatterjee
26	9789355388957	Electromagnetic Waves	Uttam M. Pal, Srijith K.
27	9789355384652	Electronic Communication	Vimal Bhatia
28	9789355388711	Embedded Systems	Santanu Chattopadhyay
29	9789355385147	Energy Science and Engineering	M. Rizwan, Majid Jamil
30	9789355387929	Engineering Economics, Estimation & Costing	Yogesh C. Joshi
31	9789355384669	Engineering Geology	R. N. Khare, Ketan Chourasia
32	9789391505066	Engineering Graphics & Design	Pradeep Jain
33	9789391505097	English (with Lab Manual)	Kulbhushan Kumar
34	9789355385963	Environmental Engineering	Chandra Sekhar Matli
35	9789355388117	Fluid Mechanics	Shreenivas N. Londhe, Pradnya R. Dixit
36	9789355388377	Fluid Mechanics & Fluid Machines	R.P. Saini
37	9789355387103	Geotechnical Engineering	Paramita Bhattacharya

UNDERGRADUATE COURSE BOOKS

S.No.	ISBN	Book Name	Author
38	9789355385130	Hydraulic Engineering	Sayantan Ganguly
39	9789355385550	Hydrology & Water Resources Engineering	Mitthan Lal Kansal, P.K. Agarwal
40	9789355389688	Information Technology Workshop in MATLAB	Hari Prabhat Gupta
41	9789355383235	Instrumentation for Civil Engineering Applications	Ashim Kanti Dey, Manita Das
42	9789355387042	Introduction to Civil Engineering	Manabendra Saharia, Nagendra R. Velaga
43	9789355384805	Introduction to Database Systems	Vikram Singh
44	9789355387509	Machine Element & System Design	Sabah Khan
45	9789355385383	Machine Learning	Himanshu Mittal
46	9789355388414	Manufacturing Automation	Chitragupt Swaroop Chitransh
47	9789355387233	Manufacturing Processes	Dheerendra Kumar Dwivedi
48	9789355389886	Materials Engineering	Dheerendra Kumar Dwivedi
49	9789391505172	Mathematics - I Calculus and Linear Algebra [For Non-Computer Science Engineering Branches]	Reena Garg
50	9789391505271	Mathematics - I Calculus and Linear Algebra [For Computer Science Engineering Branches]	Reena Garg
51	9789355384607	Measurements & Metrology	V.P. Chandramohan
52	9789355383730	Mechanics of Materials	Arvind Vyavahare
53	9789355383358	Mechatronics, Robotics & Control	J. Srinivas
54	9789355385116	Microprocessor and Microcontroller	Saurabh Chaudhury, Risha Mal
55	9789355386083	Microprocessors	Yogendra Kumar Gupta
56	9789355389169	Mobile Communication and Networks	Vimal Bhatia
57	9789355385475	Operating Systems	Sukomal Pal
58	9789355385604	Operating Systems	Sanjaya Kumar Panda
59	9789391505134	Physics (Oscillations, Waves and Optics) With lab manual	A.B. Bhattacharya, Atanu Nag
60	9789391505257	Physics (Quantum Mechanics for Engineers) With lab manual	A.B. Bhattacharya, Atanu Nag
61	9789391505165	Physics (Introduction to Electromagnetic Theory) (with Lab Manual)	A.B. Bhattacharya, Atanu Nag
62	9789391505059	Physics (Introduction to Mechanics) (with Lab Manual)	A.B. Bhattacharya, Atanu Nag
63	9789355385956	Power Electronics: Theory and Practicals	Lalit Chandra Saikia
64	9789355384942	Power Systems-I	Suresh Mikkili
65	9789355386236	Power Systems-II	Arun Rahul S, Manas K. Jena
66	9789355383754	Product Innovation & Entrepreneurship	Vigneswaran C
67	9789355384584	Production & Operation Management	Navin Kumar Dev
68	9789391505219	Programming for Problem Solving (with Lab Manual)	R.S. Salaria
69	9789355385451	Signals and Systems	Sanjay L. Nalbalwar
70	9789355386021	Strength of Materials	Uday Shanker Dixit, Nelson Muthu, S. M. Kamal
71	9789355383792	Structural Engineering	T.D. Gunneswara Rao, D. Ravi Prasad
72	9789355387004	Surveying and Geomatics	P. K. Garg
73	9789355384317	Testing & Evaluation of Civil Engineering Materials	Sandeep Chaudhary, Kashyap A Patel
74	9789355382306	Theory of Computation	Debi Prasanna Acharjya
75	9789355384928	Transportation Engineering	A.K. Raji
76	9789355385208	VLSI Design	Mahendra Sakare, Shonal Chouksey
77	9789391505332	Workshop / Manufacturing Practices (with Lab Manual)	Veeranna D.K.

S.No.	ISBN
1	9789355382481
2	97893553855
3	978935538
4	9789355
5	97893
6	978
7	
8	

DIPLOMA COURSE BOOKS

S.No.	ISBN	Book Name	Author
1	9789355382481	Aanandam An Act of Community Service	Shuchi Sharma
2	9789355385567	Advanced Manufacturing Processes	Ranjeet Kumar Sahu, Devendra Laxman Kamble
3	9789355385109	Advanced Surveying: Theory & Practice	Ramakant Agrawal, Parshottam Sarathe
4	9789355384546	Algorithms	Piyoosh P, Arnab Sarkar
5	9789391505448	Applied Chemistry (with Lab Manual)	Anju Rawlley, Devdatta Vinayakrao Saraf
6	9789391505431	Applied Physics-I (with Lab Manual)	Vinod Kumar Yadav, Mina Talati
7	9789391505578	Applied Physics-II (with Lab Manual)	Hussain Jeevakhan
8	9789355387530	Basic Mechanical Engineering	Dharmendra Singh, Chandra Shekhar Rajoria
9	9789355387394	Building Construction	Rinku Kumar, Sandeep Panchal
10	9789355383280	Building Electrification	Arnab Ghosh
11	9789355384379	Building Planning and Drawing	Aparna Dwivedi
12	9789391505493	Communication Skills in English	Anjana Tiwari
13	9789355383570	Computer Aided Machine Drawing Practice	Kanak Kalita
14	9789355388964	Computer Networking and Data Communication	Sanjaya Shankar Tripathy
15	9789355382986	Computer Networks: Theory & Practicals	Brijendra Pratap Singh, Manoj Madhava Gore
16	9789355382672	Computer Programming: Theory and Practicals	Satyendra Singh Chouhan
17	9789355387714	Computer System Organization	Sonal Yadav
18	9789355382658	Concrete Technology: Theory and Practice	Sasankasekhar Mandal, Vishwajit Anand, Sushil K. Agarwala
19	9789355383334	Construction Materials and Testing	Vanita Aggarwal
20	9789355383501	Consumer Electronics	Amit M. Joshi, Maulin M. Joshi, Urvashi Prakash Shukla
21	9789355387684	Data Structures: Theory & Practicals	NB Venkateswarlu
22	9789355388513	Design of Machine Elements	A. Kumaravel, M. Kathirselvam
23	9789355388360	Design of Steel and RCC Structure	Sparsh Johari
24	9789355383303	Digital Communication	Muralidhar Kulkarni, K. S. Shivaprakasha
25	9789355387295	Digital Electronics	Menka Yadav
26	9789355389435	Electric Circuits and Networks	Jamuna K., Nilanjan Tewari
27	9789355388452	Electric Motors and Transformers (Theory and Practicals)	Sanjay B. Bodkhe
28	9789355385901	Electric Power Transmission and Distribution	Sudhir Sharma
29	9789355389466	Electrical & Electronics Measurements and Instrumentation	Sudarsan Sahoo, Vipin Chandra Pal, Sudipta Chakraborty
30	9789355382696	Electronic Communication	M. D. Selvaraj, P. Nagaradjane
31	9789355387202	Electronic Devices and Circuits	Ankesh Jain
32	9789355386373	Electronic Equipment Maintenance	Chanchal Sharma
33	9789355384690	Embedded Systems	Deepa M, G. Santhanamari, Susithra. N
34	9789355384867	Energy Conservation and Audit	M. Rizwan, Majid Jamil
35	9789391505509	Engineering Graphics	Sharad K. Pradhan, K.K. Jain
36	9789391505608	Engineering Mechanics (with Lab Manual)	Bhankhar Bharat, Gokaldas Vandana Somkuwar

DIPLOMA COURSE BOOKS

S.No.	ISBN	Book Name	Author
37	9789391505516	Engineering Workshop Practice	A. K. Sarathe
38	9789391505653	Environmental Science	Subrat Roy
39	9789355384966	Estimating, Costing and valuation	Sandeep Panchal
40	9789355389510	Fluid Mechanics & Hydraulic Machinery	Suman Chakraborty, Sourav Mitra, Aditya Bandopadhyay
41	9789391505592	Fundamentals of Electrical and Electronics Engineering (with Lab Manual)	Susan S. Mathew, Saji T. Chacko
42	9789355387240	Fundamentals of Power Electronics	Soumitra Kumar Mandal
43	9789355389602	Geotechnical Engineering (Theory & Practicals)	Neelima Satyam
44	9789355386137	Induction, Synchronous, and Special Electrical Machines	K. Selvajyothi, S. Tamilselvi, Sarat Kumar Sahoo
45	9789355382290	Industrial Engineering & Management	A. Manimaran
46	9789355384959	Internet of Things	Sujata Pal
47	9789355388650	Introduction to DBMS: Theory & Practicals	Myneni Madhu Bala
48	9789355384294	Introduction to e-Governance	Kamal Kant Verma
49	9789355386564	Introduction to Electric Generation Systems	Lalit Chandra Saikia, Nalin Behari, Deb Choudhury
50	9789391505585	Introduction to IT Systems (with Lab Manual)	Prashant Joshi
51	9789355382900	Linear Integrated Circuit	B. T. Krishna
52	9789355388148	Manufacturing Engineering	Santosh Kumar
53	9789355383877	Material Science & Engineering	Vinod Kumar, Nisheeth k. Prasad
54	9789391505424	Mathematics-I	Deepak Singh
55	9789391505523	Mathematics-II	Garima Singh
56	9789355385994	Measurements and Metrology	A. Gnanavelbabu, M. Santhana kumar, R. Saranraj
57	9789355388131	Mechanics of Materials and their Testing	R. Velmurugan, Pragathi
58	9789355385048	Microcontroller Applications	Ritula Thakur
59	9789355385062	Microcontrollers and Applications	Santanu Chattopadhyay
60	9789355388100	Mobile and Wireless Communication	Maulin Joshi, Urvashi P. Shukla
61	9789355387790	Production & Operations Management	Mayank Kumar Agrawal
62	9789355388704	Public Health Engineering	Rinku Kumar
63	9789355387455	Python Programming	Rupesh Nasre
64	9789355387189	Renewable Energy Technologies	Sanjay Agrawal, Rajeev K. Mishra
65	9789355387479	Software Engineering	Salman Abdul Moiz
66	9789355389749	Theory of Machines & Mechanisms	G. C. Mohan Kumar
67	9789355387332	Theory of Structures	Arunachalam Subramanian Balu
68	9789355389015	Thermal Engineering - I	V. Raghavan
69	9789355389831	Thermal Engineering - II	Parvesh Antil
70	9789355386779	Transportation Engineering (Theory & Practice)	A.K. Raji, K.K. Babu
71	9789355384287	Water Resource Engineering (Theory & Practice)	Prakash C. Swain, Dillip K. Ghose
72	9789355383051	Web Technologies: Theory & Practical	Raman Dugyala

BOOKS ARE ALSO AVAILABLE IN

HINDI | MARATHI | TAMIL | BENGALI | GUJARATI

Also available as an ebook

For Detailed Catalogue, Please Scan QR Code

3.2.5 Determination of Shear Strength 53
3.2.5.1 Direct Shear Test 53
3.2.5.2 Vane Shear Test 53
Unit Summary 54
Exercises 54
Practicals 57
Know More 61
References and Suggested Readings 61

4. Bearing Capacity of Soil 63-82
Unit Specifics 63
Rationale 63
Pre-requisites 63
Unit Outcomes 63
4.1 Bearing Capacity of Soil 64
4.1.1 Basic Definitions 64
4.1.1.1 Ultimate Bearing Capacity (q_u) 64
4.1.1.2 Net Ultimate Bearing Capacity (q_{nu}) 64
4.1.1.3 Net Safe Bearing Capacity (q_{ns}) 64
4.1.1.4 Gross Safe Bearing Capacity (q_s) 65
4.1.1.5 Net Safe Settlement Pressure (q_{np}) 65
4.1.1.6 Net Allowable Bearing Pressure (q_{na}) 65
4.1.2 Terzaghi's Bearing Capacity Theory 65
4.1.2.1 General Shear Failure 66
4.1.2.2 Local Shear Failure 66
4.1.2.3 Punching Shear Failure 67
4.1.3 Effect of Water Table on Bearing Capacity 67
4.1.3.1 Condition 1: Water Table Located Above the Base of Footing 67
4.1.3.2 Condition 2: Water Table Located Below the Base of Footing 67
4.1.3.3 General Expression 68
4.1.4 Settlement of Foundation 68
4.1.5 Field Methods for Determination of Bearing Capacity 69
4.1.5.1 Plate Load Test 69
4.1.5.2 Bearing Capacity from Standard Penetration Test 71
4.2 Earth Pressure Theories 72
4.2.1 Different Types of Lateral Earth Pressure 73
4.2.1.1 At-rest Pressure 73
4.2.1.2 Active Pressure 75
4.2.1.3 Passive Pressure 75
4.2.2 Rankine's Earth Pressure Theory 75
4.2.2.1 Active Earth Pressure 75

4.2.2.2 Passive Earth Pressure 77
Unit Summary 78
Exercises 78
Know More 82
References and Suggested Readings 82

5. Compaction and Stabilization of Soil 83-102
Unit Specifics 83
Rationale 83
Pre-requisites 83
Unit Outcomes 83
5.1 Compaction 84
5.1.1 Light Compaction 84
5.1.2 Heavy Compaction 85
5.1.3 Plotting Compaction Curvc 85
5.1.3.1 Zero Air Void Line 86
5.1.3.2 Compaction Curve for Cohesion Less Sands 88
5.1.4 Factors Affecting Compaction 88
5.1.4.1 Water Content 88
5.1.4.2 Amount of Compaction 89
5.1.4.3 Method of compaction 89
5.1.4.4 Type of Soil 89
5.1.4.5 Addition of Admixtures 89
5.1.5 Suitability of Various Compaction Equipment 89
5.1.5.1 Roller 89
5.1.5.2 Rammer 90
5.1.5.3 Vibrator 90
5.1.6 Difference Between Compaction and Consolidation 90
5.2 Soil Stabilization 90
5.2.1.1 Mechanical Stabilisation 91
5.2.1.2 Cement Stabilisation 91
5.2.1.3 Lime Stabilisation 91
5.2.1.4 Bitumen Stabilisation 91
5.2.1.5 Chemical Stabilisation 92
5.2.1.6 Stabilisation by Heating 92
5.2.1.7 Electrical Stabilisation 92
5.2.1.8 Reinforced Earth and Geosynthetics 92
5.3 California Bearing Ratio (CBR) Test 92
5.4 Site Investigations 94
5.4.1 Preliminary Steps 94
5.4.2 Soil Exploration 94

5.4.2.1 Direct Methods 95
5.4.2.2 Semi-Direct Methods 95
5.4.2.3 Indirect Methods 95
5.4.2.4 Planning an Exploration Programme 95
5.4.3 Field Identification of Soils 96
5.4.3.1 Dispersion Test 97
5.4.3.2 Dilatancy Test 97
5.4.3.3 Dry Strength Test 97
5.4.3.4 Toughness Test 97
Unit Summary 97
Exercises 97
Practicals 99
Know More 101
References and Suggested Readings 101

Appendices **103**

References for Further Learning **104**

CO and PO Attainment Table **105**

Index **106-107**

1 Overview of Geology and Geotechnical Engineering

UNIT SPECIFICS

Through this unit we shall discuss the following aspects:

- Introduction of Geology and its branches
- Importance of Geology for civil engineering structure and composition of the earth
- Definition of a rock: Classification based on their genesis, and formation.
- Classification and engineering use of igneous, sedimentary and metamorphic rocks.
- Importance of soil as construction material in civil engineering structures and as foundation bed for structures.
- Field application of geotechnical engineering for foundation design, pavement design, design of earth retaining structures, design of earthen dam

RATIONALE

This overview unit on Geology and Geotechnical Engineering helps the students to get the basic information about both the subject areas. It explains the branches of geology and their significance in civil engineering applications. Knowledge about the load-bearing earth is fundamental for any construction activities. Different types of rocks, their formation, and their uses are discussed in detail, with application-level examples. Both rock and soil and very crucial construction materials and have wide applications in the field of civil engineering. The practical significance of geotechnical engineering is also discussed. The understanding of soil mechanics principles is required in multiple applications like foundation design, pavement design, retaining structures, and earthen dams.

Geotechnical engineering is an important branch of civil engineering, which deals with both soil and rock, which are fundamental construction materials. The subjects provided an idea of the engineering behaviour of both soil and rock, and their application as construction material, and foundation material.

PRE-REQUISITES

Nil

UNIT OUTCOMES

List of outcomes of this unit is as follows:

U1-O1: Understand the need for geology in civil engineering.

U1-O2: Understand the process of origin of rocks and soils.

U1-O3: Understand the types of rocks and their uses.

U1-O4: Realize the role of soil and rock as construction materials.

U1-O5: Understand the different practical applications of geotechnical engineering.

Unit-1 Outcomes	EXPECTED MAPPING WITH COURSE OUTCOMES (1- Weak Correlation; 2- Medium correlation; 3- Strong Correlation)				
	CO-1	CO-2	CO-3	CO-4	CO-5
U1-O1	3	-	-	-	-
U1-O2	3	1	1	-	-
U1-O3	3	-	-	-	-
U1-O4	1	3	1	2	-
U1-O5	1	3	2	2	1

1.1 GEOLOGY

The word 'Geology' has two parts; 'geo' which means earth and 'logy' which means 'study of', which is derived from the 'logos' meaning word or knowledge. Thus, geology is simply the study of the earth, and it deals with the composition, origin, and structure of the earth. Geology peeks deep into the time, to explain the changes that the earth surface has undergone in millions of years.

1.1.1 Branches of Geology

1.1.1.1 Physical Geology

Physical geology is the branch of geology that deals with the activity of forces, both external and internal, that shape and change the earth's crust. This branch is also known as dynamic geology.

1.1.1.2 Petrology

Petrology is the study of rocks that deals with their composition, texture, and structure; their occurrence and distribution; and their origin in relation to physicochemical conditions and geologic processes.

1.1.1.3 Mineralogy

Mineralogy is the branch of geology that covers the crystallography, description, physical, chemical and environmental features of all minerals.

1.1.1.4 Structural Geology

Structural geology is the branch of geology that is concerned with the deformation of rocks and rock formations. It aims at understanding the 3-dimensional geological architecture, from observation of the landscape and the geology visible at its surface.

1.1.1.5 Stratigraphy

Stratigraphy is the branch of geology that studies the layers (strata) of rock and layering (stratification).

1.1.1.6 *Palaeontology*

Palaeontology is the scientific study of life in the geologic past that involves the analysis of plant and animal fossils, including those of microscopic size, preserved in rocks.

1.1.1.7 *Economic Geology*

Economic geology is concerned with earth resources that can be utilized for commercial or industrial growth. Finding new ore deposits for extraction and comprehending how ore deposits are created and localized within the Earth's crust are often associated with economic geology.

1.1.1.8 *Engineering Geology*

Engineering geology is the branch of geology dealing with the application of geological knowledge to engineering problems. This involves applying the knowledge of geology to ensure the safety, economy, and efficacy of engineering projects.

1.1.2 Importance of Geology in Civil Engineering

Engineering geology can be generally defined as the study concerned with the properties of materials such as soil and rocks used in engineering projects, including the quantitative assessment. Understanding engineering geology is crucial for civil engineers as it enables them to properly plan a project. Knowledge in geology aids in ensuring a safe and economical design for building projects. Getting geological data for a project site is crucial for planning, designing, and building an engineering project. Construction activities have large financial investments, and they are closely related to the geological environment. Geological components like soil and rock are the ultimate load- carrying members in any civil engineering project, and the success of the project depends upon the understanding of the geological problems and their solutions.

The development activities of any country depend upon its major infrastructure projects, and engineering geology has a major role to play in the construction of dams, tunnels, bridges, railways, and many other major works. An engineer with a geological background is required for quality monitoring of construction materials like sand, gravel, or crushed rocks. For major projects, it is essential to understand the type of rocks present in a given location. Project planning can also be aided by geological maps. Incorporating relevant solutions if geological characteristics like faults, joints, beds, folds, or channels are discovered is an essential step of any civil engineering project. Geological maps include details on the location of different rock types in a proposed area and should be evaluated along with the topographical maps.

Before starting any project, detailed geological investigations should be carried out, to understand the geological attributes that may create construction problems. Detected site issues should be further recorded and communicated with the engineers, to adopt suitable corrective measures, and to design a stable structure. The mutual cooperation of engineering geologists and civil engineers in contributing their knowledge is highly desired for the successful completion of any civil engineering work.

1.2 ROCKS

"Crust" describes the outermost shell of a terrestrial planet. Earth's crust is generally divided into older, thicker continental crust and younger, denser oceanic crust. Earth's crust is composed of different types of rocks. The type of rock and its properties are very crucial for engineering applications, as they are used as a construction material as well as the load carrying member in foundations. The engineering properties of rocks depend upon the way of origin of rocks. Based on their origin, rocks are classified into three major groups, igneous, sedimentary, and metamorphic.

1.2.1 Igneous Rocks

Igneous rocks are formed by the cooling and solidification of hot fluid mass called magma, that exists in the interior part of the earth. During volcanic eruptions, the molten rock or magma from the earth's interior is forced out to the surface as lava. Thus, magma can get cooled and solidified either inside the earth or at the surface of the earth. Based on this, igneous rocks are classified into two, as intrusive and extrusive igneous rocks. Extrusive rocks are formed on the surface of the earth from lava, and Intrusive rocks are formed from magma that cools and solidifies within the crust of the planet.

The composition of igneous rocks can vary greatly depending on the magma they cool from. Depending on their cooling circumstances, they may also have a varied appearance. For instance, depending on how fast or slowly they cool, two identical rocks from the same magma can either become rhyolite or granite. When magma cools slowly, the crystals will be larger. When magma is located deep within the earth, the process of cooling is very slow, and the resulting rock has a coarse-grained structure. When magma rises to the surface, the temperature and pressure variations result in cooling, and the process is faster at locations closer to the surface. This results in fine to medium-grained rock formations near the surface of the earth.

When extrusive rocks are formed very near to the surface of the earth, rapid cooling provides no time for crystallization and will result in the formation of very fine textured rock, similar to glass. As they originated from the rapid cooling of lava, they are called volcanic rocks.

Fig. 1.1: Examples of igneous rocks

The engineering applications of igneous rocks range from aggregates to table tops and foundation material. Some of the most widely used igneous rocks and their applications are discussed below:

Granite is one of the most common igneous rocks, widely used for engineering applications. Granite is medium to coarse-grained, light-colored rock with a white or pink tint. The rock possesses very high strength, is hard and durable, and is suitable as a construction material. Granite outcrops act as excellent foundation materials, and the rock is reshaped for multiple applications like countertops, paving stone, floor tiles, stair treads, curbing, building veneer, and cemetery monuments. Peninsular India, eastern India, and the central Himalayas have a significant presence of granites.

Charnockites are also igneous rocks, which were first found in India. They are named after Job Charnock and are very similar to granite in terms of physical and mechanical properties. They differ from granite in terms of mineralogical composition. Eastern Ghats, Western Ghats, and Nilgiris have charnockite deposits, which are highly suitable as constriction materials, and such rocks were used for construction since ancient times. Many historical sites in India, including the Madura Meenakshi Temple in Tamil Nadu and Padmanabha Swami Temple in Kerala were built using Charnockite. Owing to its high strength and durability, charnockite is a good material for construction activities including basement stone.

Gabbro is a basic igneous rock that is coarse-grained, consisting of feldspar and ferromagnesian minerals. Fresh gabbro chips can be used for the construction of roads and other purposes. In stone industry, gabbro is named as "black granite". It is widely used for applications such as ashlars, curbing and paving stones. It is also crushed to be used as a base material in construction projects such as pavements. Upon weathering, the mineral composition of gabbro changes, and the rock becomes weak. Hence weathered or altered gabbro is not used for construction activities.

Dolerite has a very similar composition as gabbro and is very hard. Owing to its hardness and capacity to hold bitumen coating, dolerite is used for multiple engineering applications, particularly for the construction of flexible pavements. They are used as coarse aggregate in concrete, granular material in road sub-base and in flush seals, and as facing stone in buildings.

Basalt is a dark-colored fine-grained rock. Basalt is used in the base course of roads, aggregate in both concrete and asphaltic pavement surfaces, ballast for railways and filter material for drainage. Basalt with higher silica content results in alkali-aggregate reaction in concrete, and hence are not used for concrete. Laterite is the weathering product from Basalt, and it is widely used in the construction of buildings and roads.

1.2.2 Sedimentary Rocks

Sedimentary rocks are formed from pre-existing rocks, which can be sedimentary, igneous, or metamorphic. All rocks are subjected to the actions of wind, water, and ice, and will undergo decay and disintegration of the rocks and will get transformed into sediments. This process is called the denudation of rocks. Such sediments are transported by different means and are deposited at different locations. The loose sediments which are getting deposited eventually get compacted, and stratified, forming sedimentary rocks. Such rocks may be composed of both clastic and non-clastic materials.

When sediments are of chemical origin, the materials are dissolved by circulating water and are carried as a solution of water bodies, and they get precipitated into the floors. After solidification, they are mixed with the remains of sea organisms, forming non-clastic sedimentary rocks. The depositional characteristics of sedimentary rocks are thus entirely different from those of igneous and metamorphic rocks, and hence they are easily distinguishable on textural grounds.

Limestone Conglomerate Gemstone

Fig. 1.2: Examples of sedimentary rocks

Sedimentary rocks are crucial in getting historical information regarding deposition and the paleo-environment. The fossils embedded within the sediments provide information on the origin of both plant and animal life. The structure of sedimentary rocks is primarily defined by bedding or stratification.

Sandstones are the most dominant type of sedimentary rock. They are available in grain sizes ranging from gravel to fine-grained sandstone and are present in layered structures. They are primarily composed of quartz, with the presence of other minerals, like feldspar, mica, and chloride. They are available in different colours such as red and grey. In India, Vindhyan sandstones with high strength and low porosity are used for construction activities and foundations.

Shale is a soft sedimentary rock with thin layers. They get easily broken along the layers, and some shales get hardened on compaction, such as slate. The particles are fine-grained, from the size of clay to silt. It is a source material in the ceramics industry to make brick, tile, and pottery. Crushing shale and heating it with limestone makes cementitious material for construction purposes.

The consolidation of rounded boulders with cementing materials results in the formation of conglomerates. If the matrix is siliceous, rock has high strength, and is hard, but clay matrix results in easily breakable porous material. Conglomerate can be used as a fill material for roads and construction. Hard rock may be cut and polished to make dimension stone.

1.2.3 Metamorphic Rocks

As the name indicates, metamorphic rocks are formed by metamorphism of pre-existing rocks under high temperature and pressure conditions, or by chemically active fluids, resulting in chemical and physical changes in the rock. Some metamorphic rocks may show remnants of the rocks from which they are formed. In this case, the rock is called xenolith.

The two most important types of metamorphism are contact or thermal metamorphism and regional metamorphism. In contact metamorphism, country rocks react with intrusive igneous bodies, causing changes in the surrounding rocks because of the heat generated from intrusion or injection of magmatic fluids. This metamorphism happens in plutonic locations (deep-seated). Regional metamorphism in large regions and cores of folded mountains are commonly observed. All major metamorphic rocks such as gneiss, schist, phyllite, and slate are formed by regional metamorphism.

Several metamorphic rocks like gneiss, laterite, slate, and quartzite are extensively used for engineering applications. Gneiss is a banded or foliated metamorphic rock, with medium to coarse-grained particles. In general, gneiss is derived from igneous rocks such as granite, but may also be from sedimentary rocks. Being very hard, gneiss is highly suitable as a foundation material.

Fig. 1.3: Examples of sedimentary rocks

Khondalite is a light-coloured para-gneiss or para-schist, composed of quartz, sillimanite, graphite, and garnet. It can be split easily, and it is found abundantly in the Eastern Ghats. Khondalites contain manganese ores and undergoes weathering easily. However, they were used for construction in the ancient times and major temples like those in Konark and Puri in India were built using khondalite.

Granulite is an even-grained rock derived from high-grade metamorphism. The rocks with coherent grains achieve high strength and are suitable for use in engineering work. They are used as decorative stones and for interior uses such as countertops, entryways, decorative aggregates, flooring, and stair treads, and for exterior uses such as building stone, paving stone and facing stone.

Schists are named according to the presence of platy or flaky minerals, for example, mica schist, talc schist, and chlorite schist. Schists generally do not have high strength and get easily split into parts. Schists are commonly used for building walls, decorative rock walls, decorative stones, and jewellery.

Slates are characterized by cleavage, called 'slaty cleavage', imposed by metamorphism. Such rocks can be separated into big, smooth surfaced sheets along these cleavage planes. Slates are hard and are suitable for foundation, but if slates are present on hill slopes, there are higher chances of sliding along the cleavage. Slate pieces are also used for building construction of walls and fences.

Quartzites mainly consist of recrystallized quartz derived from the metamorphism of sandstone. Quartzites are very hard and durable and are good foundation material.

Marble is the metamorphic equivalent of limestone. Calcite is the major composite in marble, and it possesses good strength, and durability and is resistant to meteoric weathering. It is susceptible to chemical erosion. Marble is well suited for building stone and decorative purposes.

Laterite is another metamorphic rock widely used for construction purposes. Laterites are porous, in tallow, red or brown colour, and are used for the construction of walls and bricks, and as foundation material. To be used as a building material, well-joined, small, globular cuirasses of laterite is highly suitable. Laterite soil is used for fills for earthen dams and embankments and foundations for pavements.

1.3 SOIL

In geotechnical engineering, 'soil' is defined as an unconsolidated material, composed of solid particles (which may consist of organic matter as well), produced by the physical and chemical disintegration of rocks. There are void spaces between soil particles, and they may be filled with air, or water, or both. Geotechnical engineering is focused on the engineering behavior of earth materials such as soil and rock and is a branch of civil engineering. Unlike geology, this branch deals with the mechanics of soil and rock.

Based on the method of formation, the soil is classified into two, residual soils and transported soils. If soil remains at the place of its formation close to the parent rock, it is called residual soil. Transported soils are found away from their place of origin, and are transported by different means, as described in Fig. 1.4 below:

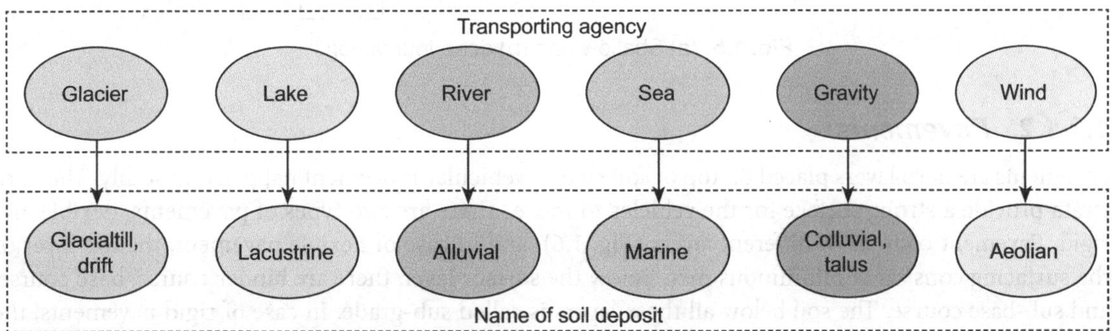

Fig. 1.4: Classification of transported soils

The use of soil as a construction material depends upon its engineering behaviour. Permeability, strength, compaction characteristics, drainage, shrink-swell potential, grain size, plasticity, and reactivity are among the features of soils that are crucial in engineering. Applications like the construction and maintenance of highways, airports, pipelines, foundations, irrigation systems, ponds, tiny dams, and systems for the disposal of sewage and trash are all impacted by these qualities to varying degrees and in different combinations. All the properties will be discussed in different chapters of this book, and some important engineering applications of soil as discussed in section 1.3.1.

1.3.1 Field Applications

Geotechnical engineering is an important branch of civil engineering, as it deals with two critical construction materials, soil, and rock. The primary function of both these materials is to act as the ultimate load-bearing strata for any applied load on the earth's crust.

1.3.1.1 Foundations

Every construction or civil engineering structure ultimately rests on the surface of the earth. Soil or rock bears the load transferred from the structure, and the foundation transfers the load from the structure to the soil. Foundations are designed after bearing capacity and settlement analysis and are classified into two, based on their depth-to-width ratio (Fig. 1.5).

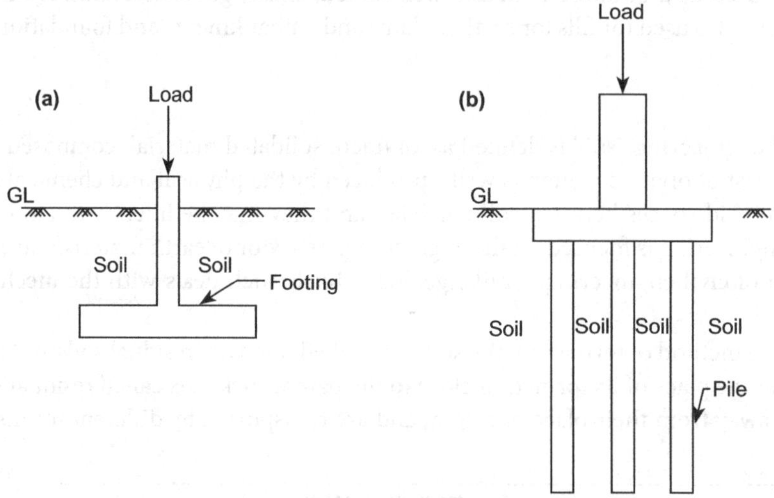

Fig. 1.5: (a) Shallow and (b) deep foundations

1.3.1.2 Pavements

Pavements are hard layers placed on top of soil so that vehicular movement happens smoothly. The hard strata provide a strong surface for the vehicles to move. There are two types of pavements, flexible and rigid. Pavement consists of different layers (Fig. 1.6), and in case of flexible pavement, the top layer or the surfacing consists of bituminous mix. Below the surface layer, there are binder course, base course, and sub-base course. The soil below all these layers is called sub-grade. In case of rigid pavements, the loads are supported through the rigidity of the material. In such pavements, a rigid slab, usually made by concrete rests on top of granular base and sub-base courses and a compacted subgrade (Fig. 1.6).

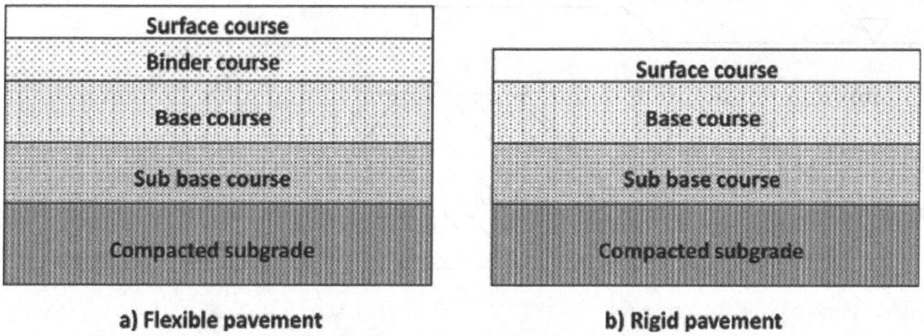

Fig. 1.6: Layers of pavement

1.3.1.3 Retaining structures

Earth retaining structures are needed to keep the soil at different elevations on either of its sides (Fig. 1.7). Retaining structures can be made of different materials, such as concrete, masonry, or sheet. Retaining structures made of sheets are known as sheet piles. Retaining structures are designed based using earth pressure theories.

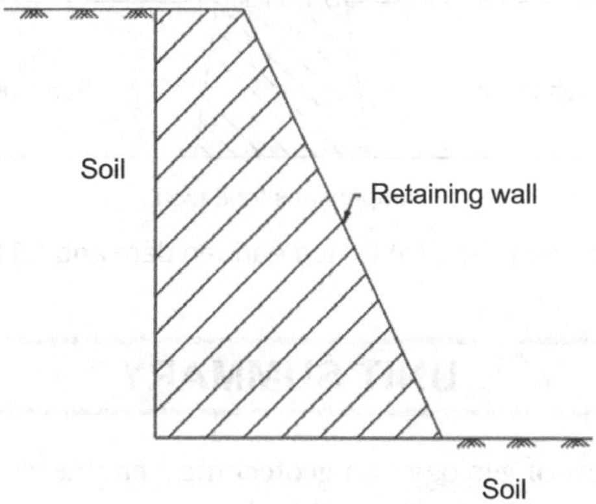

Fig. 1.7: Retaining wall

1.3.1.4 Earthen dam

Earthen dams are large structures in which soil is used as a construction material. They are constructed for creating water reservoirs. The design of earthen dams requires thorough knowledge of geotechnical engineering, and it uses the concepts of seepage through the soil, and slope stability. Based on the section, earthen dams are classified as homogeneous, zoned, and diaphragm-type as shown in Fig. 1.8.

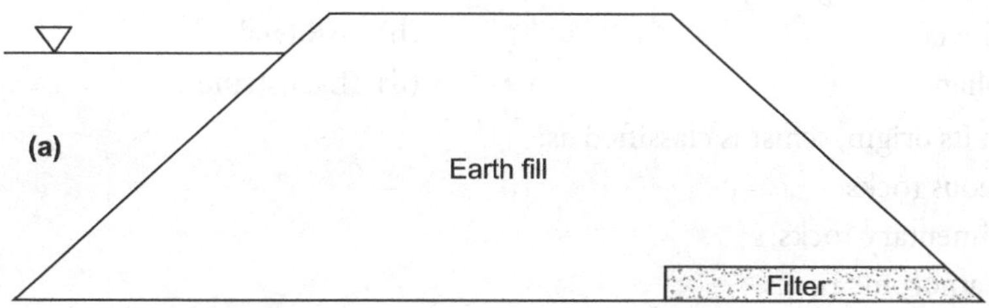

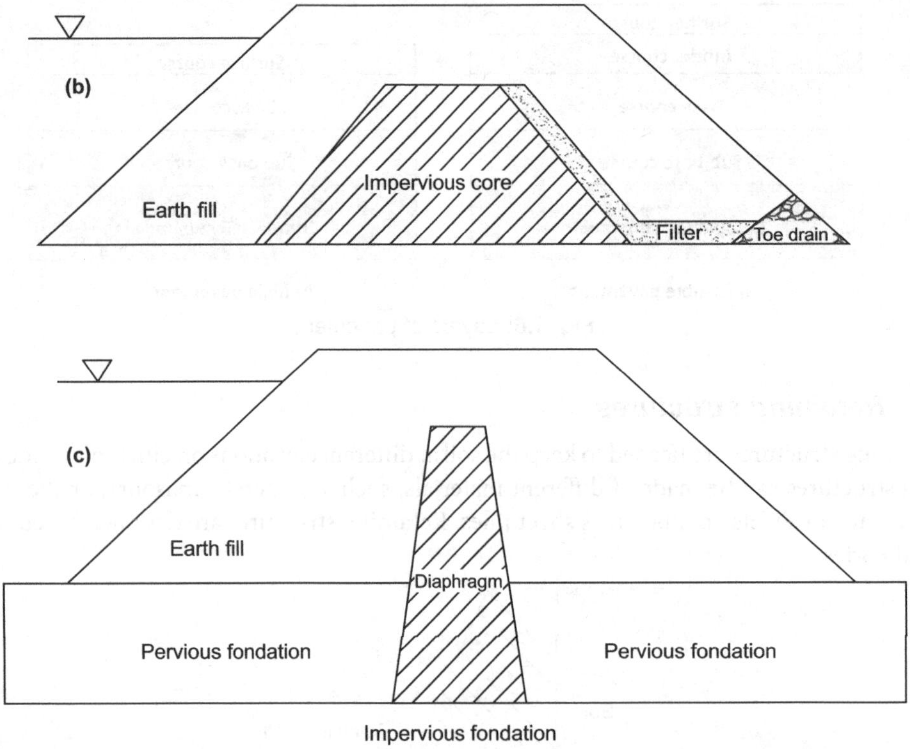

Fig. 1.8: (a) Homogenous earthen dam, (b) Zoned earthen dam and (c) Diaphragm-type earthen dam

UNIT SUMMARY

The unit discusses the overview of geology and geotechnical engineering. The types of rocks and their engineering applications are discussed along with the significance of geology in civil engineering. Further, the types of soil and the field applications of geotechnical engineering are discussed.

EXERCISES

Multiple Choice Questions

1. Soil transported by gravity is called:
   (a) Colluvial
   (b) Alluvial
   (c) Aeolian
   (d) Lacustrine
2. Based on its origin, schist is classified as:
   (a) Igneous rocks
   (b) Sedimentary rocks
   (c) Metamorphic rocks

3. The branch of geology that deals with the layers of soil is known as:
   (a) Engineering geology (b) Palaeontology
   (c) Stratigraphy (d) Structural geology
4. Which of the following rocks are least suitable as a foundation material
   (a) Granite (b) Shale
   (c) Gneiss (d) Quartzite

Answers of Multiple Choice Questions			
1. (a)	2. (c)	3. (c)	4. (b)

Short and Long Answer Type Questions

1. What are intrusive and extrusive igneous rocks?
2. State whether the sentence is true or false and justify your answer.
   "Slate formations along slopes are highly suitable."
3. What is metamorphism?
4. What is meant by a retaining structure?
5. What are the different branches of geology?
6. Describe the engineering applications of different igneous rocks.
7. How will geological knowledge help in civil engineering projects?
8. Explain the classification of rocks based on their origin, with examples.
9. What are the major roles of soil in construction projects? Explain with examples.
10. Draw the figure of a zoned earthen dam and mark the parts.

PRACTICALS

Name of experiment: Identification of rocks from the given specimen

Aim: To identify the type of rock, using visual inspection

Theory: Based on their origin, rocks are classified into igneous, sedimentary and metamorphic. These rocks can be distinguished from each other using visual inspection, using their structure and texture. Structure depends on the basic characteristics and spatial arrangement of the main components of the rock, whereas texture depends on the dimensions, form, and connections of the minerals (mineral aggregates). If they are volcanic, igneous rocks have a vesicular structure, an amygdaloidal structure, or an aphanitic structure. If they are hypabyssal or plutonic, they are compact, thick, and have a texture that interlocks. Sedimentary rocks are characterized by the presence of regular or crossbedding, cementing material, fossils, ripple marks, mud cracks, footprints and trails, and unusual shapes. Based on colour, grain size, texture, hardness, and other physical characteristics, different beds can be distinguished. The presence of metamorphic minerals and the alignment of minerals (lineation, foliation) indicate the presence of the metamorphic group of rocks.

Observations:

Colour:

Grain:

Texture or structure:

Result:

Rock type:

Inference:

KNOW MORE

Malpasset Dam Failure, France, 1959

Malpasset Dam was a double-curvature concrete arch dam that spanned across the Reyran River in Southern France. It was constructed in 1954, and failed on 2nd December, 1959.

Malpasset dam, left, at end of construction, summer 1954 (photo COB); right, soon after failure, end 1959 (photo Mary) (Daffaut, 2013)

Explore the reasons behind the failure. The case study will provide you with insights on the importance of geology and geotechnical engineering in civil engineering projects.

REFERENCES AND SUGGESTED READINGS

- Chenna Kesavulu N., Textbook of Engineering Geology, Trinity Press, Benguluru
- Duffaut, P. (2013, 5:5). The Traps Behind the Failure of Malpasset Arch Dam, France, in 1959. Journal of Rock Mechanics and Geotechnical Engineering, 335-341.
- Gangopadhyay S., Engineering Geology, Oxford University Press, New Delhi

Dynamic QR Code for Further Reading

2 Physical and Index Properties of Soil

UNIT SPECIFICS

Through this unit we shall discuss the following aspects:

- Soil as a three-phase system
- Water content - definition and determination as per IS code
- Unit weight of soil- laboratory experiments
- Particle size distribution
- Consistency of soil
- Soil classification

RATIONALE

This unit on the physical and index properties of soil provides a brief introduction to the constituents of soil. First, the three different phases in soil are explained, along with the weight volume relationships. The engineering behaviour of soil is very complex, as it varies with time, according to the water content and arrangement of particles. The volume relationships, unit weight and specific gravity are critical in all earthwork applications. The engineering behaviour of soils can also be understood from the index properties of soil. Index properties are those which are not primarily engineering properties but are indicative of engineering properties. For larger- sized particles, particle size distribution and relative density are the main index properties, while for fine-grained particles, important index properties are obtained from the Atterberg limits.

PRE-REQUISITES

Nil

UNIT OUTCOMES

List of outcomes of this unit is as follows:

U2-O1: Understand the constituents of soil and three phase system.

U2-O2: Understand the volumetric relationships and volume-weight relationships in the three- phase system.

U2-O3: Learn the laboratory experiments to determine the water content and unit weight of soil.

U2-O4: Understand the particle size distribution and consistency limits of soils.

U2-O5: Learn to classify the soil based on grain size distribution and consistency limits.

Unit-2 Outcomes	EXPECTED MAPPING WITH COURSE OUTCOMES (1- Weak Correlation; 2- Medium correlation; 3- Strong Correlation)				
	CO-1	CO-2	CO-3	CO-4	CO-5
U2-O1	2	3	-	-	-
U2-O2	2	3	-	-	-
U2-O3	2	3	-	-	-
U2-O4	1	3	-	-	-
U2-O5	1	3	-	-	-

2.1 SOIL AS A THREE-PHASE SYSTEM

Soil is a mixture of solids, air, and water, which constitutes the three phases of soil. The solid phase exists as particulate material of varying sizes, and the void spaces in between are filled with either air or water or both. When all the voids are filled with air, the soil is said to be in dry condition, and when water occupies all the void spaces, the soil is said to be in a fully saturated condition.

2.1.1 Three Phase Diagrams

Three phase diagram is the graphical representation of different phases in soil. The dry state, partially saturated state, and fully saturated state can be represented graphically as shown in Fig. 2.1.

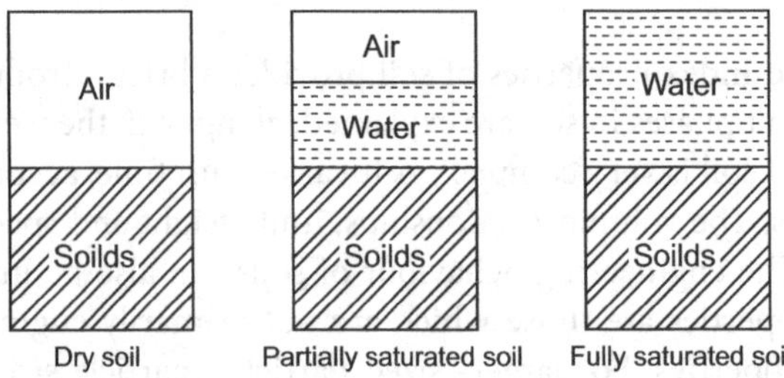

Fig. 2.1: Phase diagrams of soil in the dry state, partially saturated state, and fully saturated state

Both dry and fully saturated conditions have only two phases, and the three-phase system is represented in Fig. 2. 2. On the left side, the volumes and on the right side, the weights are written. While "V" represents volume, "W" represents weight. The subscripts 'v', 'a,' 'w' and 's' represents voids, air, water and solids respectively.

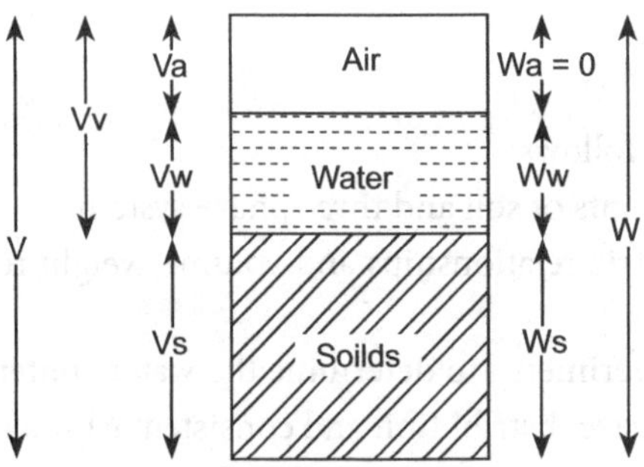

Fig. 2.2: Three-phase diagram

The total volume of the soil sample always remains constant, but the weight of the sample varies according to the amount of water in void spaces. The different volumetric relationships in the three-phase system are as follows:

2.1.1.1 Void Ratio (e)

Void ratio is the ratio of the volume of voids to the volume of solids in a soil mass.

$$e = \frac{V_v}{V_S} \tag{2.1}$$

2.1.1.2 Porosity (n)

Porosity is the ratio of the volume of voids to the total volume of soil mass.

$$n = \frac{V_v}{V} \tag{2.2}$$

2.1.1.3 Degree of Saturation (S)

Degree of saturation is the ratio of the volume of water to the volume of voids in the soil mass.

$$S = \frac{V_W}{V_V} \tag{2.3}$$

2.1.1.4 Percent Air Voids (n_a)

Percent air voids is defined as the ratio of the volume of air to the total volume of soil mass.

$$n_a = \frac{V_a}{V} \tag{2.4}$$

2.1.1.5 Air Content (a_c)

Air content is the ratio of the volume of air to the volume of voids in the soil mass.

$$n_a = \frac{V_a}{V} \tag{2.5}$$

2.1.2 Water Content

Water content or moisture content of a soil mass is defined as the ratio of the weight of water to the weight of solids in the soil mass.

a_c

$$w = \frac{W_w}{W_s} \tag{2.6}$$

The water content of the soil is a critical parameter that controls the engineering behaviour of soil. The following are some methods used to determine the water content:

- Oven drying method
- Pycnometer method

- Torsion balance method
- Sand bath method
- Calcium carbide method
- Alcohol method
- Rapid moisture meter

Oven drying is the most widely followed laboratory method for the determination of water content. This is highly accurate but requires a duration of 24 hours to get the results. In the field, water content is determined by rapid moisture meter, sand bath method, alcohol method, or calcium carbide method.

2.1.3 Unit Weight of Soil

The unit weight, also known as the 'weight density, of a soil refers to its weight per cubic metre and is typically expressed as kilonewtons per cubic metre (kN/m³), or tons per cubic metre (t/m³). Unit weight is a crucial parameter required for geotechnical design and volume estimation of earthworks. The water content, particle composition, and degree of compaction all affect the unit weight. Based on the water content and submergence, different unit weights of soil are defined as follows:

2.1.3.1 Bulk Unit Weight (γ)

Bulk unit weight is the total weight of soil per unit volume, and is given by:

$$\gamma = \frac{W}{V} \tag{2.7}$$

2.1.3.2 Dry Unit Weight (γ_d)

Dry unit weight is the weight of solids per unit weight of soil.

$$\gamma_d = \frac{W_S}{V} \tag{2.8}$$

2.1.3.3 Saturated Unit Weight (γ_{sat})

When the soil is fully saturated, the bulk unit weight is termed as saturated unit weight.

$$\gamma_{sat} = \frac{W_{sat}}{V} \tag{2.9}$$

2.1.3.4 Submerged Unit Weight (γ_{sub})

If the soil exists below the groundwater table, it is said to be in submerged condition. The unit weight in this condition will be the buoyant weight per unit volume of soil.

$$\gamma_{sub} = \frac{W_{sub}}{V} \tag{2.10}$$

This value is also equal to the difference between the saturated unit weight of soil and the unit weight of water.

$$\gamma_{sub} = \gamma_{sat} - \gamma_w \tag{2.11}$$

The unit weight of water at 4°C is 1 g /ml or 9.81 kN/m³.

2.1.3.5 *Unit Weight of Soil Solids*

Unit weight of soil solids is the ratio of the weight of solids to the volume of solids in a soil mass.

$$\gamma_s = \frac{W_s}{V_s} \tag{2.12}$$

In laboratory and field conditions, the bulk unit weight is measured using the following approaches:

- Water displacement method
- Submerged weight method
- Core cutter method
- Sand replacement method
- Water balloon method

Core cutter is a field method, suitable for soft and fine-grained soils, while the sand replacement is the most widely followed approach, for all soil types. The water balloon method is also suitable for all soil types. Once the bulk unit weight is determined, dry unit weight can be calculated using the following equation:

$$\gamma_d = \frac{\gamma}{1+w} \tag{2.13}$$

2.1.4 Specific Gravity

In general, specific gravity is termed as the ratio of unit weight of any material to the unit weight of water. In case of soil, two values of specific gravity are used, which are mass specific gravity and true specific gravity.

2.1.4.1 *Mass or Bulk specific Gravity (G_m)*

Mass specific gravity is defined as the ratio of bulk unit weight of the soil to the unit weight of water, given by:

$$G_m = \frac{\gamma}{\gamma_w} \tag{2.14}$$

2.1.4.2 *True or Absolute Specific Gravity or Specific Gravity of Soil Solids (G)*

True specific gravity is the ratio of the unit weight of soil solids to the unit weight of water.

$$G = \frac{\gamma_s}{\gamma_w} \tag{2.15}$$

Specific gravity is determined in the laboratory using the following approaches:

- Density bottle method
- Pycnometer method
- Measuring flask method
- Gas jar method
- Shrinkage limit method

2.1.5 Inter Relationships

Among the discussed parameters, water content, unit weight and specific gravity are determined directly in the laboratory, and the other parameters are derived using inter-relationships between the parameters. These relationships are listed below in Table 2.1.

Table 2.1: Inter-relationships

S. No.	Relationship
1.	$n=\frac{e}{1+e}$
2.	$e=\frac{n}{1-n}=\frac{G-G_m}{G_m-S}$
3.	$n_a=n.a_c=1-\frac{(1+wG)\gamma_d}{G\gamma_w}$
4.	$S+a_c=1$
5.	$eS=wG$
6.	$\gamma=\frac{(G+eS)\gamma_w}{1+e}=\frac{(1+w)G\gamma_w}{1+e}$
7.	$\gamma_d=\frac{\gamma}{1+w}=\frac{G\gamma_w}{1+e}=\frac{(1-n_a)G\gamma_w}{1+wG}$
8.	$\gamma_{sat}=\frac{(G+e)\gamma_w}{1+e}$
9.	$\gamma_{sub}=\frac{(G-1)\gamma_w}{1+e}$

2.2 PARTICLE SIZE DISTRIBUTION

Soil particles are mechanically separated based on their particle size. The particles of size greater than 75 μm, are called coarse grained soil, and their separation is carried out using sieve analysis. The particles with size less than 75 μm are called fine grained soils, and their particle size distribution is carried out using sedimentation.

Based on the size, soils are classified into gravels (>4.75 mm), sand (4.75 mm > particle size > 75 μm), silt (75 μm > particle size > 2 μm) and clay (< 2 μm).

2.2.1 Laboratory Analysis

Sieve analysis is carried out by arranging sieves of different sizes in decreasing order (largest one on top), and by shaking (manually, or using a mechanical shaker). The particles retained on each sieve is then measured to plot the grain size distribution curve. The sieve analysis is done separately for particles greater than 4.75 mm and those in between 4.75 mm and 75 μm.

For fine grained soil, sedimentation analysis is carried out based on Stoke's law, either using a pipette, or using a hydrometer.

When the soil mass consists of both coarse- and fine-grained particles, first the particles are washed to separate the fine particles attached to the larger ones. Sieve analysis is then carried out for the larger particles, and sedimentation for fine particles, and the final particle size distribution is obtained from the combined analysis. This process is called wet sieve analysis.

2.2.2 Particle Size Distribution Curve

The particle size distribution curve is the graphical representation of particle sizes in a soil mass. It is a plot between the percentage of soil mass finer than a given size on y-axis, and the particle size on log scale in x-axis.

The distribution of particles of different sizes in a soil mass is called grading, and it can be determined from the particle size distribution curve. The particle size distribution curves for different soils are plotted below in Fig. 2.3

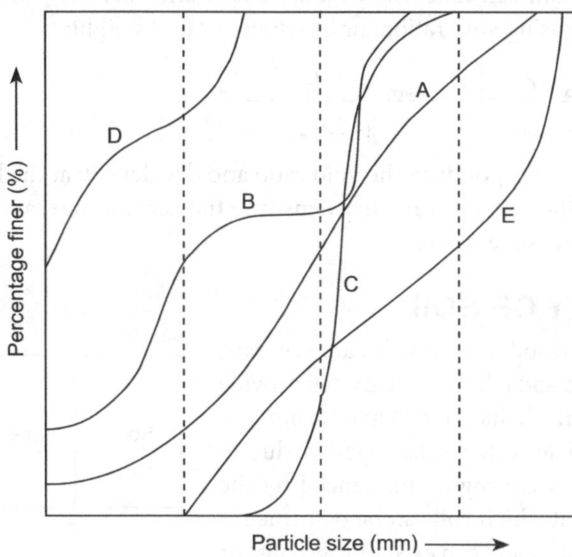

Fig. 2.3: Particle size distribution curves

The curve A is a flat S curve, which implies that the mass consists of particles of different size in good proportion. Such soils are call well graded soil. In such soils, the space between larger particles will be occupied by smaller particles, and the void space will be minimum. Curve with intermediate flat portions as in B represents gap graded soil, where particles of intermediate size are missing. Very steep S curves like C represents uniformly graded soil, in which particles are of similar size. Curves like D on the left upper side of the graph represents fine particles, and as the curve shifts right, it indicates that the particles are of larger size.

Two important coefficients are calculated from the particle size distribution curve, which are known as the uniformity coefficient (C_u), and coefficient of curvature (C_c). While C_u expresses the uniformity of the soil, the general shape is described by C_c. These coefficients can be calculated from the plot as:

$$C_u = \frac{D_{60}}{D_{10}} \tag{2.16}$$

$$C_c = \frac{(D_{30})^2}{D_{60} \times D_{10}} \tag{2.17}$$

where D_{60} is the particle size such that 60% of the soil is finer than this size, and similarly D_{30} and D_{10} are the particle sizes such that 30% and 10% of the particles are finer than this size respectively. D_{10} is also called the effective size. Higher values of C_u indicate that the particle sizes are largely varying. Gravels are considered well graded when they have a C_u value greater than 4, and a C_c value between 1 and 3. In the case of sand, C_u greater than 6 and C_c between 1 and 3 are considered as the criteria for well graded soil. If any of these criteria are not satisfied, the soil is considered to be poorly graded.

2.2.3 Relative Density

Relative density is another important index property of coarse-grained soils. It is also known as density index. This parameter indicates how the soil will behave under loads. Higher relative density indicates that the soil mass is dense and can take heavy loads. The relative density can be calculated using the following expression, either using void ration, or by using dry unit weight:

$$D_r or\ I_D = \frac{e_{max} - e}{e_{max} - e_{min}} = \left[\frac{(\gamma_d)_{max}}{\gamma_d}\right]\left[\frac{\gamma_d - (\gamma_d)_{min}}{(\gamma_d)_{max} - (\gamma_d)_{min}}\right] \tag{2.18}$$

where e_{max} and $(\gamma_d)_{min}$ corresponds to the void ratio and dry density at the loosest state of soil, e_{min} and $(\gamma_d)_{max}$ corresponds to the void ratio and dry density at the densest state, and and are the void ratio and dry density at the natural state of soil.

2.3 CONSISTENCY OF SOIL

In the case of coarse-grained soil, the particles are separate, and particle size distribution and relative density can provide indications on the engineering behaviour. When it comes to fine- grained soil, the particles often stick together due to cohesion, and the properties are highly influenced by the moisture content. The ease at which soil can be deformed is known as consistency. The same soil can exist in solid state or can behave like a liquid with variation in water content. This range from liquid solid was divided into four distinct states by Swedish Engineer Atterberg in 1911. The four stages are separated by three moisture contents, which are known as the Atterberg limits or consistency limits (Fig. 2.4).

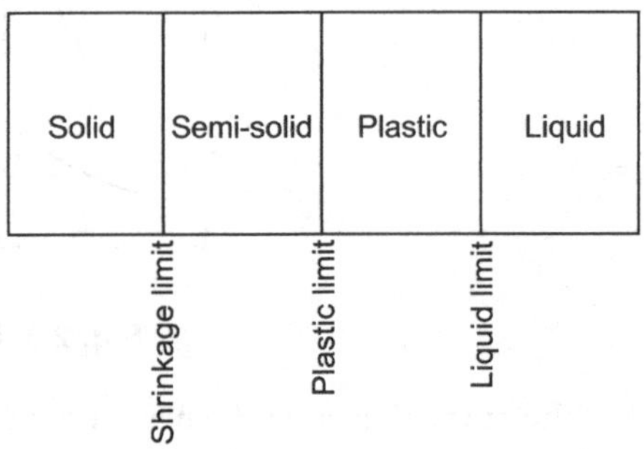

Fig. 2.4: Atterberg limits

2.3.1 Atterberg Limits

2.3.1.1 *Liquid limit (w_l)*

Liquid limit is the water content at which soil changes from plastic to liquid state. It is defined as the water content at which a soil pat in the standard liquid limit apparatus cut by a groove of standard dimensions will flow together for a distance of 12 mm under impact of 25 blows of standard height.

2.3.1.2 Plastic Limit (w_p)

Plastic limit is defined as the minimum water content at which soil just begin to crumble when rolled into a thread of approximately 3 mm in diameter.

2.3.1.3 Shrinkage Limit (w_s)

Shrinkage limit is the maximum water content at which a reduction in water content will not cause a decrease in the soil volume.

2.3.1.4 Plasticity Index (I_P)

Plasticity index is the range of water content over which the soil remains in the plastic state. It can be calculated as the difference between liquid limit and plastic limit.

$$I_P = w_l - w_p \tag{2.19}$$

2.3.1.5 Shrinkage Index (I_s)

The shrinkage index is the numerical difference between plastic limit and shrinkage limit.

$$I_s = w_p - w_s \tag{2.20}$$

2.3.1.6 Liquidity index (I_l)

Liquidity index is the ratio of the difference between natural water content and the plastic limit, to the plasticity index.

$$I_l = \frac{w - w_p}{w_l - w_p} \tag{2.21}$$

If the value of I_l is greater than 1, the soil is in liquid state, and if the value is less than zero, soil is in semi solid state. Any value between 0 and 1 indicates that the soil is in plastic state.

2.3.1.7 Consistency Index (I_c)

Consistency index is defined as the ratio of the difference between liquid limit and the natural water content to the plasticity index of soil.

$$I_c = \frac{w_l - w}{w_l - w_p} \tag{2.22}$$

If the value of consistency index is greater than 1, it means that the soil is in semi-solid state, and if the value is less than 0, the soil is in liquid state.

The consistency of soil in the field can be stated based on the values of I_l and I_c as listed in Table 2.2.

Table 2.2: Consistency classification

I_c	I_l	Consistency
1.00 to 0.75	0.00 to 0.25	Stiff
0.75 to 0.50	0.25 to 0.50	Medium stiff
0.50 to 0.25	0.50 to 0.75	Soft
0.25 to 0.00	0.75 to 1.00	Very soft

2.3.1.8 *Flow Index (I_f)*

The flow index is the slope of the flow curve drawn between the number of blows (log scale) on x axis and the water content along y axis in Cassagrande's method of liquid limit determination (Fig. 2. 5).

Mathematically, I_f can be calculated as:

$$I_f = \frac{w_1 - w_2}{\log_{10}\left(\frac{N_2}{N_1}\right)} H \tag{2.23}$$

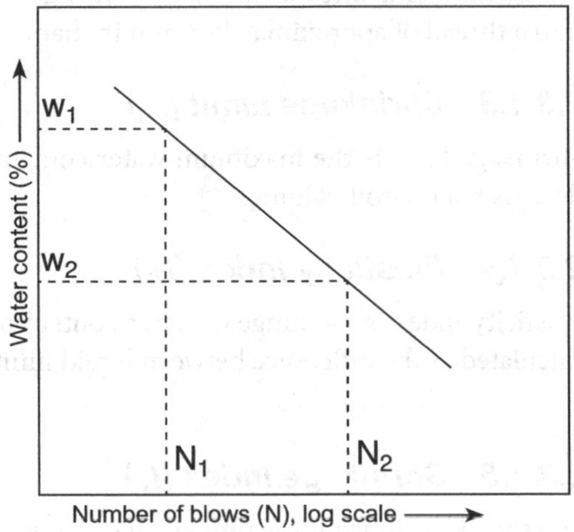

Fig. 2.5: Flow curve

2.3.1.9 Toughness Index *(I_t)*

Toughness index can be defined as the ratio of plasticity index and flow index.

$$I_t = \frac{I_p}{I_f} \tag{2.24}$$

2.3.1.10 *Sensitivity*

In the case of clayey soil, the strength properties are highly related to the structure of clay, which is the orientation and arrangement of particles. When samples are remoulded, it affects the strength of soil. Sensitivity (S_t) is defined as the ratio of unconfined compressive strength of soil in undisturbed condition to that in remoulded condition, without any change in the water content. Unconfined compressive strength (q_u) is obtained by providing axial compressive load to a cylindrical soil sample, which is laterally unsupported. The test procedure will be discussed in the further sections.

$$S_t = \frac{(q_u)_{undisturbed}}{(q_u)_{remoulded}} \tag{2.25}$$

Clays are considered to be sensitive if the value of sensitivity is greater than 4.

2.3.1.11 *Activity*

Minerals present in clay also have a very significant role on the engineering properties of soil. Activity is an indirect index of effect of clay minerals in a soil sample, using its plasticity index and amount of clay present in the sample, as mentioned in the following equation:

$$A = \frac{I_p}{F} \tag{2.26}$$

where F is the percentage of clay fraction in the soil sample. A clayey sample is considered to be active when the value of activity is greater than 1.25.

2.3.1.12 *Thixotropy*

Thixotropy is the change due to touch. Soil loses its strength while remoulding due to rearrangement of particles and disturbance caused to water molecules. Some of these changes can be reversed with time.

When a remoulded soil sample stays without loss of water, it regains some part its strength, and this process of regaining strength with time after remoulding is known as thixotropy.

2.4 CLASSIFICATION OF SOILS – IS CLASSIFICATION SYSTEM

Soil classification categorises different types of soils into groups according to their engineering behaviour. IS 1498:1971 (Reaffirmed in 2007) is the Indian Standard that deals with the classification and identification of soils for general engineering purposes. Based on this classification system, soils are broadly classified into 3, coarse grained soil, fine grained soils and highly organic soils and other miscellaneous materials. When more than 50 % of the material (by weight) is retained on a 75 μm sieve, soil is called coarse grained soil, and if more than 50 % of the material (by weight) is passing through 75 μm sieve, the soil is classified as fine grained.

Organic soil and other miscellaneous soil materials consist of large percentages of organic matter such as decomposed vegetation, and peat. In addition, soils containing other materials like cinders, shells and non-soil materials are also grouped under this category.

Coarse grained soils can be further classified into gravels and sand, and the classification is shown in Fig. 2.6.

The first letter indicates the particle size which is present in the maximum quantity. For coarse grained soils, it is always G or S, representing gravel or sand respectively. The second letter represent whether the soil is well graded or poorly graded, if the soil has no significant fine fraction. When fine fraction is present, the second letter represents either clay (C) or Silt (M), based on the plasticity chart (Fig. 2.7), or dual symbols can be used. GW is termed as well graded gravel, and GC is termed as clayey gravel.

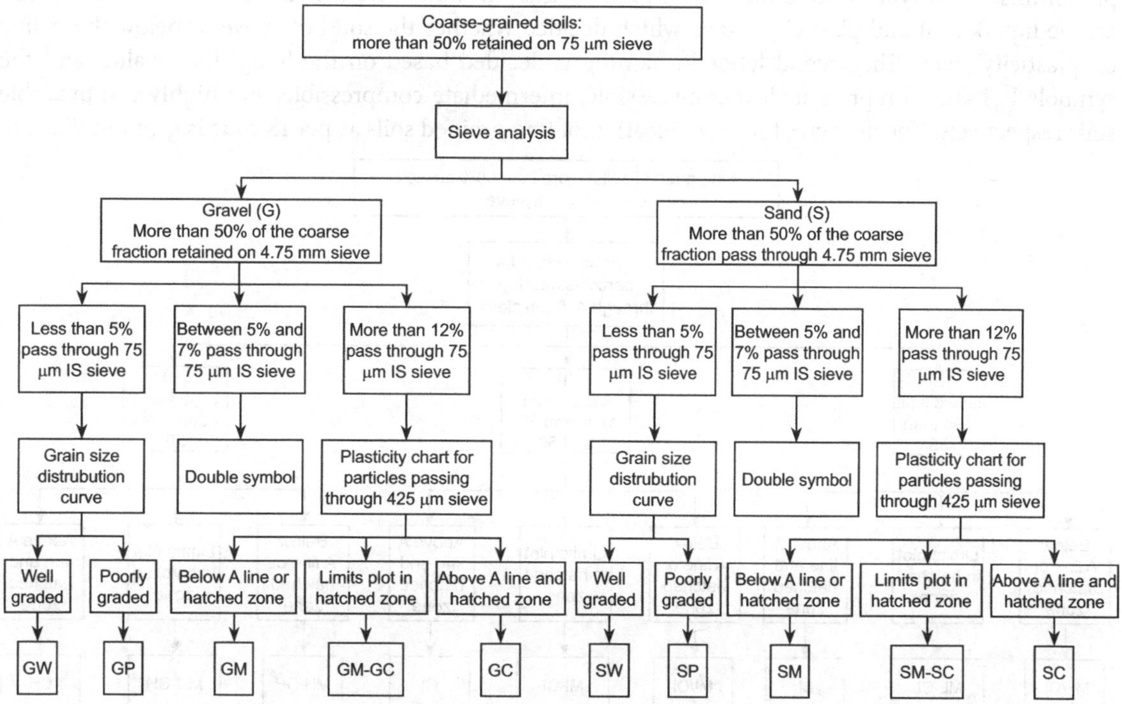

Fig. 2.6: Flow chart for classification of coarse-grained soils

In the case of fine grained soils, plasticity chart plays a key role in the classification. The plasticity chart as per IS classification is shown in Fig. 2.7.

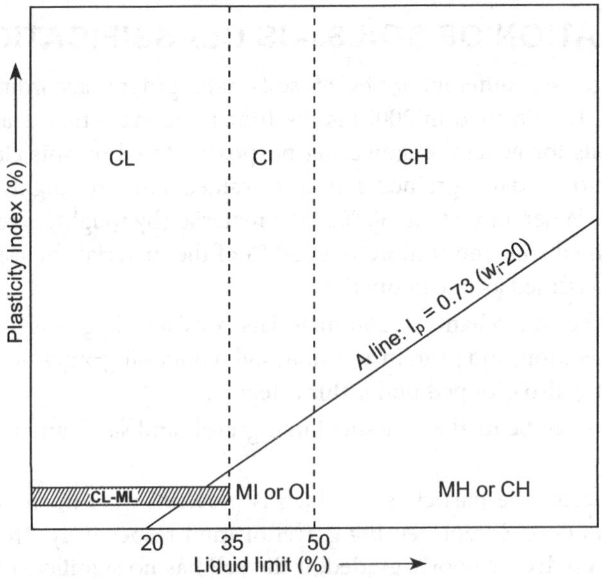

Fig. 2.7: Plasticity chart and IS soil classification.

Similar to coarse grained soils, the first letter in the case of fine-grained soil also represent the predominant soil type. Unlike the coarse-grained classification, here the first letter is decided based on the liquid limit and plasticity index, which decided whether the soil lies above or below the A line on plasticity chart. The second letter in naming is decided based on the liquid limit value, and the symbols L, I and H represents low compressible, intermediate compressible, and highly compressible soils respectively. The flow chart for classification of fine-grained soils as per IS code is given in Fig. 2.8.

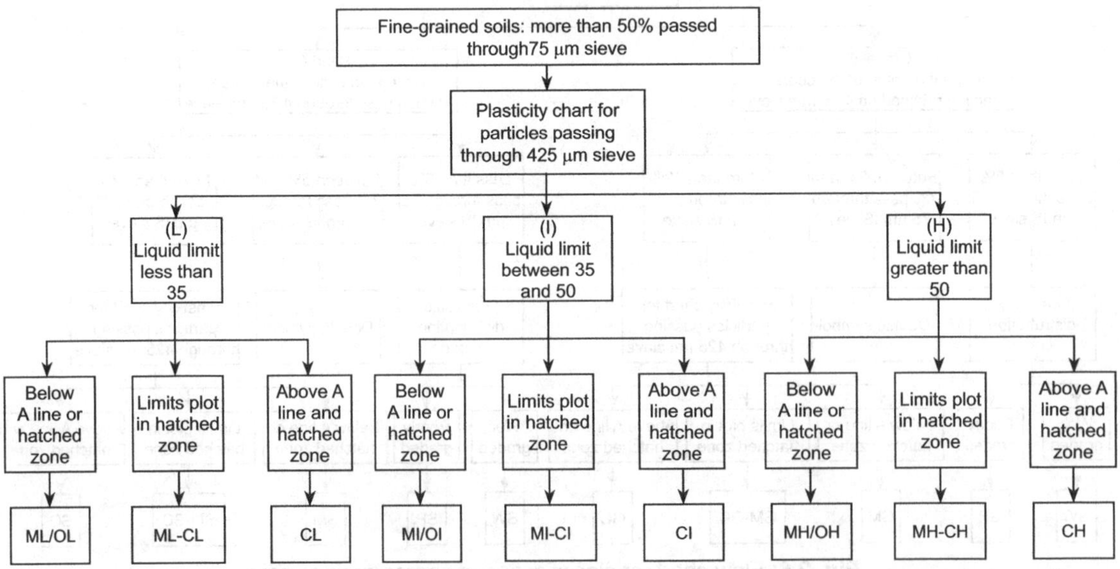

Fig. 2.8: Flow chart for classification of fine-grained soils

UNIT SUMMARY

The unit discusses the physical and index properties of soils. Starting from the three-phase system, the volumetric and weight volume relationships are discussed in detail. Further, the index properties and soil classification are explained, to help the student understand how soil should be categorised for engineering application, based on Indian Standards.

EXERCISES

Multiple Choice Questions

1. The ratio of the volume of voids to the total volume of soil is-
   (a) Voids ratio (b) Degree of saturation
   (c) Porosity (d) Air content
2. The soil which plots above the 'A' line in the plasticity chart are-
   (a) Silts (b) Clays
   (c) Sands (d) Organic soils
3. At shrinkage limit, the soil is-
   (a) Saturated (b) Partially saturated
   (c) Dry (d) None of the above
4. A saturated soil sample has a bulk unit weight of 19 kN/m^3 and a specific gravity of 2.68. Determine the water content of soil?
   (a) 0.166 (b) 0.3
   (c) 0.143 (d) 0.277

Answers of multiple Choice Questions			
1. (c)	2. (b)	3. (a)	4. (c)

Numerical Examples

1. A partially saturated soil sample collected from an earth fill has a natural moisture content of 23 % and a unit weight of 19.6 kN/m^3. If the specific gravity of the soil is 2.65, calculate
   a. Void ratio
   b. Degree of saturation
   c. Saturated unit weight

$$w = 23\ \%$$

$$\gamma = 19.6\ \mathrm{kN/m^3}$$

$$\gamma = \frac{(1+w)G\gamma_w}{1+e}$$

$$e = \frac{(1+w)G\gamma_w}{\gamma} - 1$$

(a) $e = \frac{(1+0.23)\times 2.65\times 9.81}{19.6} - 1 = 0.63$

(b) $S = \frac{wG}{e} = \frac{0.23\times 2.65}{0.63} = 0.97$

(c) $\gamma_{sat} = \frac{(G+e)\gamma_w}{1+e} = \frac{(2.65+0.63)\times 9.81}{1+0.63} = 19.74\%$

2. A soil sample in dry state weighs 400 g and has a volume of 250 cm³. Calculate the shrinkage limit and void ratio of the sample if the specific gravity is 2.67.

$$\rho_d = \frac{M_s}{V}$$

$$\rho_{d=1.6\,g/cc}$$

$$\rho_d = \frac{G\rho_w}{1+e}$$

$$e = \frac{2.67\times 1}{\rho_d} - 1 = 0.67$$

$$\rho_s = G\rho_w = \frac{M_s}{V_s}$$

$$V_s = \frac{M_s}{G\rho_w} = \frac{400}{2.67\times 1} = 149.81 cm^3$$

$$M_w = V_w\rho_w = 100.19\ g$$

$$Shrinkage\,limit = \frac{M_w}{M_s} = \frac{100.19}{400} = 25.05\%$$

Exercises:

1. The liquid limit and plastic limit of a soil sample are 55% and 25% respectively. If the natural water content of the soil is 32%, calculate the consistency index and the liquidity index?

($I_c = 0.6, I_l = 0.24$)

2. A soil sample has a bulk unit weight of 19.88 kN/m³ at a moisture content of 16 %. Calculate the moisture content of the soil if the unit weight becomes 18.42 kN/m³ after drying, while the voids ratio remains unchanged.

(w=7.48%)

3. A clayey soil sample has liquid limit 51% and plastic limit 33%.
   (a) In what state of consistency is this soil at a moisture content of 44%?
   (b) What is the plasticity index of the soil?
   (c) The void ratio of this soil at the minimum volume reached on shrinkage, is 0.78. What is the shrinkage limit, if its grain specific gravity is 2.61?

{(a) Plastic state (b) I_p = 18% (c) w_s= 29.88 %}

4. A clay sample with a specific gravity of 2.68 has void ratio of 0.50 in the dry condition. Determine the shrinkage limit of this clay?

(w_s =18.65%)

5. The liquid limit and plastic limit of a clayey soil sample are 60% and 35%, respectively. From a particle size distribution curve, it was observed that the sample consists of 60% of particles smaller than 0.002 mm. What is the activity of soil?

(A = 0.41)

Short and Long Answer Type Questions

1. Explain Atterberg limits for soil and their necessity?
2. Define the terms specific gravity and density index.
3. Differentiate between sieve analysis and sedimentation analysis.
4. What is the function of plasticity chart in soil classification?
5. What is the significance of effective size of particle in sieve analysis.
6. Explain in detail the procedure for determination of grain size distribution of a soil sample containing both coarse and fine particles.
7. Write down the procedure for determining specific gravity of a given soil in the laboratory by using a pycnometer.
8. What is meant by the term "index properties of soils"? What is their importance?
9. What do you understand by the consistency of soil? How is it determined?
10. What do you understand by the three-phase system of soil? Explain with a neat sketch.

PRACTICALS

Name of experiment: Determination of water content of by oven drying method (IS 2720) **Aim:** To determine the water content of the given soil sample by oven drying method **Apparatus required:** Weighing balance (Accuracy 0.01 g), desiccators, containers, oven.

Theory: Water content is defined as the ratio of mass of water to mass of solids in a given sample. Water content is one of the most important factors that determine the engineering behaviour of soil, as the strength parameters of any soil sample depends upon its moisture content.

Procedure:

1. Take an empty container and measure its mass ('*W*1' g).
2. Collect the wet soil sample and put it in the container.
3. Measure the mass of container filled with wet soil sample ('*W*2' g).
4. Keep the filled container in thermostatically controlled oven at a temperature 105 °C- 110 °C for 24 hours, so that water will get evaporated completely.
5. Take out the container from oven and cool it in desiccators for 5 minutes.
6. Measure the mass of container with dry soil ('*W*3' g).
7. Calculate the water content as $w = (W2- W3) / (W3- W1) \times 100$.
8. Repeat all above steps two more times to calculate average water content of given soil sample.

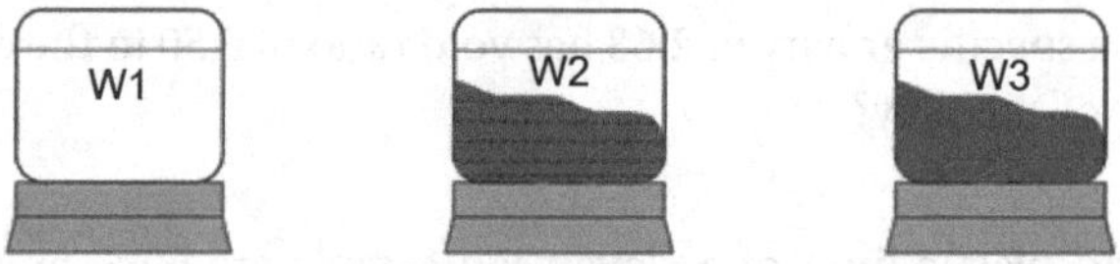

Observations:

Container No.	Sample 1	Sample 2	Sample 3
Mass of empty container with lid ($W1$) g			
Mass of container with lid and wet soil ($W2$) g			
Mass of container with lid and dry soil ($W3$) g			
Mass of water ($W_w = W2 - W3$) g			
Mass of dry soil ($W_s = W3 - W1$) g			
Water content in % w = $(W_w / W_s) \times 100$			

Result:

Inference:

Name of experiment: Determination of density of soil by core cutter method (IS 2720)
Aim: To determine the bulk density and dry density of soil by core cutter method
Apparatus required: Core cutter with dolly, measuring scale, weighing balance, oven, containers
Theory: Bulk Density of Soil (γ) is defined as the ratio of bulk mass of soil to the volume of soil. $\gamma = (W / V) = [(Ws + Wv) / V]$; where Ws = mass of soil solids and Wv = mass of voids (Weight of water). Dry Density of Soil (γd) is defined as the ratio of dry mass of soil to the volume of soil. $\gamma d = (Wd / Vd) = (Ws / V)$. In core cutter method, the density is determined by using a core cutter, which is inserted into the ground. The density of soil in the field is then calculated by using the mass of soil contained in the core cutter.

Procedure:

1. Measure the height (h) and internal diameter (d) of the core cutter and calculate its volume.
2. Weigh the empty core cutter without dolly as ($W1$) g.
3. Clean and level the location where density is to be determined.
4. Drive the core cutter, with a steel dolly on its top, into the soil to its full depth with the help of a steel rammer, so that half of dolly will remain above the ground.
5. Excavate the soil around the cutter with a and gently lift the cutter filled with soil.
6. Weigh the core cutter with filled with soil ($W2$), after trimming the top and bottom surfaces of the sample and cleaning the outside surface of the cutter

7. Calculate bulk density of field soil as $\gamma = (W2 - W1) / V$
8. Remove the soil from the core cutter, using a sample extractor and take representative soil sample from it to determine the moisture content using any one method as w%.
9. Calculate dry density of field soil as $\gamma d = (\gamma) / (1 + w)$
10. Repeat all above steps two more locations in the field to determine average dry density of soil.

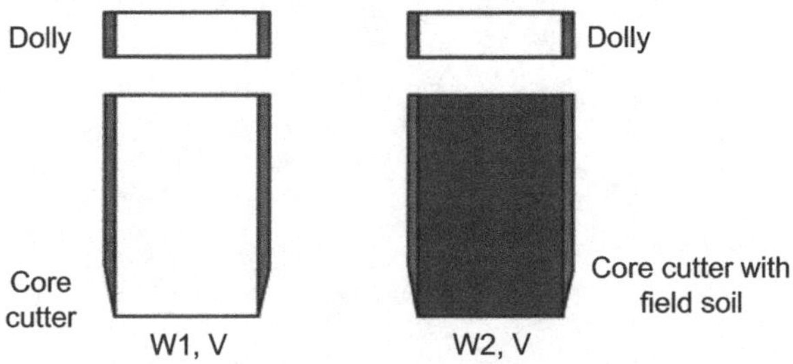

Observations:

Internal diameter of core cutter d = ... cm.

Height of core cutter h = ... cm.

Volume of core cutter V = ... cm³.

	Sample 1	Sample 2	Sample 3
	Determining density of sand		
Mass of empty core cutter ($W1$) g			
Mass of core cutter filled with field soil ($W2$) g			
Bulk Density of soil $\gamma = (W2 - W1) / V$, g /cc.			
	Water content		
Container No.			
Mass of empty container with lid ($w1$) g			
Mass of container with lid and wet soil ($w2$) g			
Mass of container with lid and dry soil ($w3$) g			
Mass of water ($ww = w2 - w3$) g			
Mass of dry soil ($ws = w3 - w1$) g			
Water content in % $w = (ww / ws) \times 100$			

	Sample 1	Sample 2	Sample 3
	Dry density		
Dry Density of soil $\gamma_d = (\gamma) / (1 + w)$, g /cc.			

Result:

Inference:

Name of experiment: Determination of density of soil by sand replacement method (IS 2720)

Aim: To determine the bulk density and dry density of soil by sand replacement method

Apparatus required: Sand pouring cylinder, calibrating container, metal tray with central hole, weighing balance, sand

Theory: Bulk Density of Soil (γ) is defined as the ratio of bulk mass of soil to the volume of soil. $\gamma = (W / V) = [(Ws + Wv) / V]$; where Ws = mass of soil solids and Wv = mass of voids (Weight of water). Dry Density of Soil (γd) is defined as the ratio of dry mass of soil to the volume of soil. $\gamma d = (Wd / Vd) = (Ws / V)$. In sand replacement method, a small cylindrical pit is excavated in the ground and the mass of excavated soil is measured. The excavated pit is then filled with sand of known density. The volume of the pit can be calculated using weight and density of the sand, and then density of insitu soil can be calculated using weight of excavated soil and volume of the pit.

Procedure:

1. Remove the cap of sand pouring cylinder, close the shutter, fill the test sand passing through 1mm and retained on 600 μm from the top.
2. Find the mass of sand pouring cylinder with sand ($W1$). Place the sand pouring cylinder over the calibration container, open the shutter and allow the sand to flow out for filling the calibration container. Close the shutter.
3. Place this sand pouring cylinder now on a clean and plane surface. Open the shutter and allow the sand to flow out for filling cone fully. Close the shutter, remove the sand pouring cylinder, collect the sand which occupied in the cone and find out its mass ($W2$).
4. Refill the sand pouring cylinder with sand such that it weighs equal to initial mass $W1$. Place the sand pouring cylinder centrally on the calibration container with volume $V1$.
5. Open the shutter and allow the sand to fill in the calibration container and cone completely. Close the shutter and find the mass of cylinder with remaining sand as ($W3$).
6. Refill the sand pouring cylinder with sand such that it weighs equal to initial mass $W1$ and take it to the field, along with metal tray and trowel.
7. Place metal tray having central hole on the prepared ground, and excavate the soil using trowel up to 150 mm (approximately) depth, remove loose soil carefully and collect it in the metal container

8. Remove the metal tray having central hole, place the sand pouring cylinder full of sand centrally over excavated pit.
9. Open the shutter and allow sand to fill in excavated pit and cone completely. Close the shutter and take it to laboratory to find the mass of cylinder with remaining sand ($W4$).
10. Find the mass of soil collected from the pit (W).
11. Determine water content of collected soil by oven drying method as w.
12. Repeat the steps two times more to get average value of dry density of field soil.

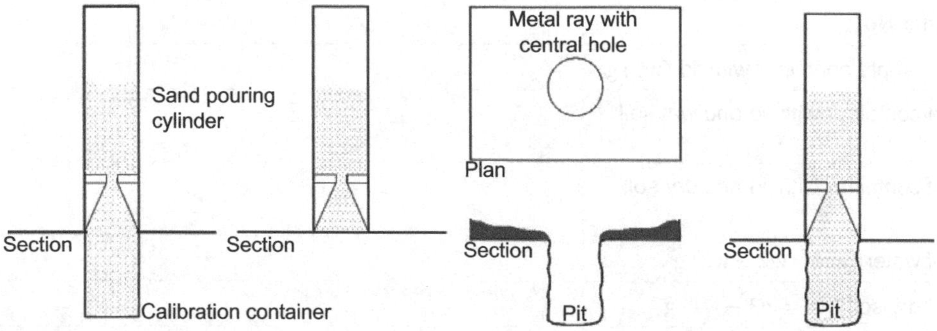

Observations:

Internal diameter of calibrating container (d) = ... cm.

Internal height of calibrating container (h) = ... cm.

Volume of calibrating container ($V1$) = ... cm^3.

	Sample 1	Sample 2	Sample 3
	Density of Sand		
Mass of sand pouring cylinder full of sand ($W1$) g			
Mass of sand in cone ($W2$) g			
Mass of cylinder after pouring sand in calibrating container and cone ($W3$) g			
Mass of sand filled In calibrating container ($Ws = W1 - W3 - W2$) g			
Density of sand ($\gamma s = Ws/V1$) g / cc			
	Density of Soil		
Mass of sand pouring cylinder full of sand ($W1$) g			
Mass of collected soil (W) g			
Mass of cylinder after pouring sand in excavated pit and cone ($W4$) g			
Mass of sand filled in excavated pit ($W5 = W1 - W4 - W2$) g			

	Sample 1	Sample 2	Sample 3
Volume of collected soil = Volume of pit = Volume of sand filled in excavated pit ($V = W5 / \gamma s$) cc			
Bulk density ($\gamma = W/V$) g /cc			
Water Content			
Container No.			
Mass of empty container with lid ($w1$) g			
Mass of container with lid and wet soil ($w2$) g			
Mass of container with lid and dry soil ($w3$) g			
Mass of water ($ww = w2 - w3$) g			
Mass of dry soil ($ws = w3 - w1$) g			
Water content in % w = (ww / ws) x 100			
Dry Density			
Dry Density of soil, γd = (γ) / (1 + w) g /cc.			

Result:

Inference:

Name of experiment: Determination of specific gravity by pycnometer method (IS 2720)

Aim: To determine the specific gravity of the given soil sample using pycnometer

Apparatus required: Pycnometer, stirrer, pipette, oven, weighing balance, wash bottle, distilled water Pycnometer

Theory: Specific gravity is the ratio of density of soil to density of water. Specific gravity is a critical parameter in the determination of void ratio and other soil properties.

Procedure:

1. Per batch Clean the pycnometer bottle and dry it. Take the weight of empty pycnometer with conical cap as '$W1$' g .
2. Oven dry the given soil sample passing through 4.75 mm and retained on 75 micron IS sieve, in oven at temperature 105-110°C for 24 hours to get dry soil.
3. Place this soil sample about 150-200 g in the pycnometer and take its weight as '$W2$' g .
4. Now add the distilled water to half of height of pycnometer and stir it well, so that entrapped air is completely removed.
5. Fill the distilled water up to top of conical cap using pipette.
6. Take the weight of pycnometer filled with distilled water as '$W3$' g.
7. Clean the pycnometer.
8. Fill the pycnometer bottle with distilled water only up to top of conical cap.
9. Take the weight of pycnometer completely filled with water as $W4$ g.
10. Calculate the specific gravity G, as $(W2 - 1) / [(W4 - W1) - (W3 - W2)]$
11. Repeat all above steps two more times to calculate average specific gravity of given soil sample.

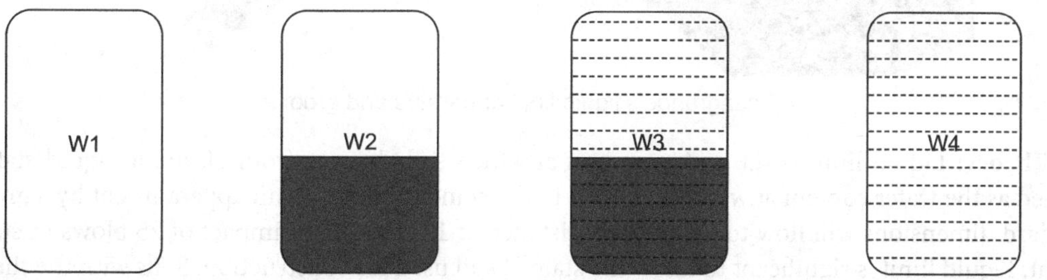

Empty pycnometer | Pycnometer with dry soil | Pycnometer with soil and water | Pycnometer with water

Observations:

Room temperature at the time of test .... °C.

	Sample 1	Sample 2	Sample 3
Mass of empty pycnometer $(W1)$ g			
Mass of pycnometer with dry soil $(W2)$ g			
Mass of pycnometer with soil and water $(W3)$ g			
Mass of pycnometer with water $(W4)$ g			
Specific Gravity $G = (W2 - W1) / ((W4 - W1) - (W3 - W2))$			

Result:

Inference:

Name of experiment: Determination of liquid limit using Casagrande's liquid limit apparatus (IS 2720)

Aim: To determine the liquid limit of the given soil sample using Casagrande's liquid limit apparatus

Apparatus required: Casagrande's liquid limit apparatus, grooving tool, IS sieve of 425 μm, mixing dishes, weighing balance, spatulas, oven

Casagrande's liquid limit apparatus and grooves

Theory: Liquid limit is the water content at which soil changes from plastic to liquid state. It is defined as the water content at which a soil pat in the standard liquid limit apparatus cut by a groove of standard dimensions will flow together for a distance of 12 mm under impact of 25 blows of standard height. Liquid limit is significant to know the state of soil used for construction. Soils with the the insitu moisture content closer to liquid limit, can be considered as soft. If the moisture is too lesser when compared to the liquid limit, the soil is stiff. Above the liquid limit, soil loses its shear strength completely and behaves lie a fluid.

Procedure:

1. Take about 120 gm of air-dried soil passing 425 μm I.S sieve.
2. The sample is then mixed with distilled water to form a uniform paste.
3. A part of this paste is then spread into the cup liquid limit device using spatula. At the point of maximum thickness, the depth of soil can be 1 cm. Excess soil has to be trimmed.
4. Divide the paste in the cup along centreline, using the grooving tool such that firm dimensions are made.
5. Turn the crank at two rpm, till the two parts of the paste join together for atleast 1 cm length, by flow, and record the number of blows.
6. If the number of blows are between 10 and 40, keep a representative sample from the cup for water content determination.
7. Repeat the test such that four readings of number of blows are obtained between 10 and 40.

Observations:

Room temperature at the time of test .... °C.

Experiment No.	Sample 1	Sample 2	Sample 3	Sample 4
Container No.				
Mass of empty container with lid ($w1$) g				
Mass of container with lid and wet soil ($w2$) g				
Mass of container with lid and dry soil ($w3$) g				
Mass of water ($ww = w2 - w3$) g				
Water content in % $w = (ww / ws) \times 100$				

Result:

Liquid limit (from graph):

Flow index:

$$I_f = \frac{w_1 - w_2}{\log_{10}\left(N_2 / N_1\right)}$$

Inference:

Name of experiment: Determination of plastic limit (IS 2720)

Aim: To determine the plastic limit of the given soil sample

Apparatus required: Porcelain dish, glass plate, weighing balance and oven

Theory: Plastic limit is defined as the minimum water content at which soil just begin to crumble when rolled into a thread of approximately 3 mm in diameter.

Procedure:

1. Sieve the given soil sample through 425 μm sieve and take about 20 gm of sample.
2. Mix the sample with distilled water thoroughly till the soil mass becomes plastic enough to be moulded with fingers.
3. Take a part of this soil and place it over the glass plate. Roll the soil between fingers and glass plate, to a thread of uniform diameter at 6 to 90 strokes per minute.
4. Continue rolling till you get a the diameter of the thread becomes 3 mm diameter.

5. If the thread does not crumble at 3 mm diameter, kneed the soil again ad roll it again on the glass plate.
6. Continue the process until the thread crumbles with 3 mm diameter.
7. Collect the pieces of the crumbled thread and determine the moisture content.
8. Repeat the test atleast three more times and express the results in the nearest whole number.

Observations:

Room temperature at the time of test .... °C.

Experiment No.	Sample 1	Sample 2	Sample 3	Sample 4
Container No.				
Mass of empty container with lid ($w1$) g				
Mass of container with lid and wet soil ($w2$) g				
Mass of container with lid and dry soil ($w3$) g				
Mass of water ($ww = w2 - w3$) g				
Water content in % $w = (ww / ws)\ x\ 100$				

Result:

Plastic limit:

Plasticity Index,

$$I_P = w_l - w_p$$

Toughness index

$$I_t = \frac{I_p}{I_f} =$$

Inference:

Name of experiment: Determination of shrinkage limit of the soil (IS 2720)

Aim: To determine the shrinkage limit of the given soil sample.

Apparatus required: Evaporating dish, spatula, shrinkage dish, straight edge, glass cup, two glass plates, IS 2 mm and 425- μm sieves, mercury, weighing balance and oven

Theory: Shrinkage limit is the maximum water content at which a reduction in water content will not cause a decrease in the soil volume. The value is highly useful in areas where soils undergo significant changes in volume.

Procedure:

1. Take about 100 gm of the soil sample from passing through 425 μm IS sieve.
2. Take a part of the soil sample in an evaporating dish and mix with distilled water till the voids are filled in.
3. Weigh the empty shrinkage dish ($W1$). Fill the paste in the shrinkage dish in three equal layers, after coating inside of the dish with a thin layer of grease or oil.
4. Weigh the shrinkage dish with wet soil as $W2$.
5. Dry the sample in air for 6 to 8h, till the colour of the sample becomes light and then in the oven at temperature 105° C to 110° C for 12 to 16 h.
6. Weigh the shrinkage dish with oven-dried soil and note as $W3$.
7. Determine the volume of shrinkage dish which is evidently equal to volume of the wet soil as follows. Take out the soil cake from the dish; keep the empty shrinkage dish in a stainless- steel cup and fill with mercury. Find the weight of shrinkage dish with full of mercury ($W4$). Use the weight of mercury to determine the volume of wet soil pat.
8. Determine the volume of dry soil pat by removing the pat from the shrinkage dish and immersing it in the glass cup full of mercury. Place the glass cup in a larger one and fill the glass cup to overflowing with mercury. Remove the excess mercury by covering the cup with glass plate with prongs and pressing it. Wipe out the outside of the glass cup. Then, place it in another larger dish, which is, clean and empty carefully. Place the dry soil pat on the mercury. It floats submerge it with the pronged glass plate which is again made flush with top of the cup. The mercury spills over into the larger plate. Measure the weight of the plate with mercury, and use the weight of mercury Ws to determine the volume of dry pat.

Observations:

Room temperature at the time of test .... °C.

	Sample 1	Sample 2	Sample 3
Weight of an empty shrinkage dish, $W1$			
Weight of the shrinkage dish with wet soil, $W2$.			
Weight of shrinkage dish with oven dried soil, $W3$			
Weight of dry soil, $Wd = W3 - W1$			
Volume of wet soil pat ($V1$), in cm^3			
Volume of dry soil pat ($V2$) in cm^3			
Shrinkage limit $w_s = \{(W2 - W3) - (V1 - V2)\gamma_w\} / (Wd) \times 100$			

Result:

Inference:

Name of experiment: Determination of particle size distribution of the given soil (IS 2720)

Aim: To determine the particle size distribution of the given soil sample using sieve analysis.

Apparatus required: IS sieves with size varying from 4.75 mm to 75 μm, weighing balance, sieve shaker.

Theory: Grain size distribution is important in classifying the soil for engineering uses. The grain size distribution determines the suitability of a soil for different applications.

Procedure:

1. I.S sieves should be arranged in the order as shown in the table.
2. The soil sample is separated into various fractions by sieving using mechanical sieve shaker for 10 minutes.
3. The weight of soil retained on each sieve is recorded (No soil particle shall be pushed through the sieves)

Observations:

Weight of soil sample:

I.S sieve number or size in mm	Weight retained in each sieve (gm)	Percentage retained on each sieve	Cumulative percentage retained	Percentage finer
4.75				
4.00				
3.36				
2.40				
1.46				
1.20				
0.60				
0.30				
0.15				
0.075				

Result:

$D10$:

$D30$:

$D60$:

Cu:

Cc:

Soil classification:

Inference:

KNOW MORE

Apart from Indian Standard classification system, other classifications also exist for engineering classification of soil. The major classification systems include Unified Soil Classification System, Textural Classification of Soil, US Bureau of Soils Classification, AASHTO System of Soil Classification, International Classification System, and Massachusetts Institute of Technology System. The primary objective of these classification systems is to provide information about the expected engineering properties of soil. Some of these classifications like Massachusetts Institute of Technology System, International Classification System, and Massachusetts Institute of Technology System use only grain size for classification, while the others use texture or plasticity characteristics also for the purpose of classification.

REFERENCES AND SUGGESTED READINGS

- Arora,K.R., "*Soil Mechanics and Foundation Engineering*," Standard Publishers Distributors, Delhi, 2008.
- Gulhati, S. K.; Datta, M." *Geotechnical engineering*, Tata McGraw-Hill, New Delhi, 2005.
- IS 2720 (Part II) – 1973 (Reaffirmed 2010): *Methods of test for soils, Part II Determination of water content.*
- IS 2720 (Part III) – 1980 (Reaffirmed 2002): *Methods of test for soils, Part III Determination of specific gravity*
- IS:2720 (Part XXVIII)-1974 (Reaffirmed 2010): *Methods of test for soils, Part XXVIII Determination of dry density of soils in-place, by the sand replacement method*
- IS:2720 (Part XXIX)-1975 (Reaffirmed 2005): *Methods of test for soils, Part XXIX Determination of dry density of soils in-place, by the core-cutter method.*

Dynamic QR Code for Further Reading

3 Permeability and Shear Strength of Soil

UNIT SPECIFICS

Through this unit we shall discuss the following aspects:

- Permeability of soil
- Darcy's law
- Factors affecting permeability
- Seepage through earthen structures
- Shear strength of soil
- Mohr-Coulomb failure theory
- Strength envelope
- Direct shear and vane shear tests

RATIONALE

This unit on the permeability and shear strength of soil provides a brief introduction to two critical properties of soil. Both permeability and shear strength are crucial when soil is considered as an engineering material. Seepage is a critical problem in all earthen structures and knowledge of permeability is critical while designing them. Shear strength is another critical engineering property of soil and is defined as the magnitude of shear stress that can be sustained by soil. Knowledge of both permeability and shear strength are required in computing the stability of soil slopes and calculating the bearing capacity of foundations.

PRE-REQUISITES

Nil

UNIT OUTCOMES

List of outcomes of this unit is as follows:

U3-O1: Learn Darcy's law of permeability and factors affecting permeability

U3-O2: Understand the process of determination of coefficient of permeability in laboratory.

U3-O3: Know different earthen structures and seepage through them.

U3-O4: Understand shear failure of soil, and components of shearing resistance.

U3-O5: Learn the laboratory tests to determine shear strength of soil.

Unit-3 Outcomes	EXPECTED MAPPING WITH COURSE OUTCOMES (1- Weak Correlation; 2- Medium correlation; 3- Strong Correlation)				
	CO-1	CO-2	CO-3	CO-4	CO-5
U3-O1	-	2	3	-	-
U3-O2	-	2	3	-	-
U3-O3	-	2	3	-	-
U3-O4	-	2	3	-	-
U3-O5	-	2	3	-	-

3.1 PERMEABILITY OF SOIL

Permeability is an important engineering property of soils. It is defined as the property of a soil which allows the flow of water (or any other fluid) through its interconnecting pores. Determination of permeability is critical in solving number of engineering problems, settlements in foundations, yield of wells, and seepage through and below the earthen structures. The hydraulic stability of a soil mass is controlled by its permeability.

3.1.1 Darcy's Law of Permeability

Among different soil types, large sized particles such as gravels are highly permeable while fine particles like clays are least permeable. When the flow of water through soils laminar, it is governed by Darcy's Law (1956). According to Darcy's law, velocity of laminar and continuous flow in a homogeneous saturated soil, the is proportional to the hydraulic gradient, and is given by:

$$v = ki \tag{3.1}$$

where, v - Velocity of flow,

k - Coefficient of permeability

i - hydraulic gradient, given by $i = \frac{h}{L}$

L - length of the sample and

h - head causing flow.

The law is formulated based on the following assumptions:

- The soil is fully saturated
- The flow is laminar
- The flow is steady and continuous
- The total cross-sectional area of soil is considered

The volume of flow per unit time or discharge (q) is obtained by multiplying v by the total cross-sectional area of both solids and voids (A).

$$q = vA = kiA \tag{3.2}$$

3.1.2 Coefficient of Permeability

Coefficient of permeability is defined as the average velocity of flow through the total cross-sectional area of soil under unit hydraulic gradient. The coefficient of permeability (k) has the dimensions of velocity, and is given by the equation:

$$k = C\left(\frac{\gamma_w}{\mu}\right)\left(\frac{e^3}{1+e}\right)D^2 \tag{3.3}$$

where C is a constant depending upon the shape of conduit, γ_w is the unit weight of water, μ is the coefficient of viscosity, e is the void ratio, and D is the diameter of the hypothetical spherical grains assumed. The coefficient of permeability depends upon the following factors:

- **Particle size:** As evident from Eq. (3.3), coefficient of permeability is proportional to the square of the diameter of particle. Coarse particles are highly permeable, while fine particles are less permeable.
- **Shape of particles:** The particle shape decides the specific surface. If the void ratio remains the same, angular particles are less permeable than rounded particles.
- **Structure of soil mass:** The coefficient C considers the shape of flow conduit, which depends on the structure of soil mass. Flocculated soil structure is more permeable than dispersed structure, at the same void ratio.
- **Properties of the pore fluid (water):** As mentioned in Eq. (3.3), coefficient of permeability is directly proportional to the unit weight of water and is inversely proportional to its viscosity coefficient. When temperature increases, the permeability increases due to decrease in viscosity.
- **Adsorbed water:** Adsorbed water is usually observed in fine grained soils, and they are immobile under the influence of gravity. This water causes obstruction to the movement of fluid through pores, and thus decreases permeability.
- Void ratio: From Eq. (3.3), it can be understood that the coefficient of permeability of a soil sample is proportional to $\frac{e^3}{1+e}$. However, the permeability of a soil at a given void ratio does not have any relationship with that of other soils with the same ratio. Even though clays have the maximum void ratio, they are the least permeable, due to the small size of void passage.
- **Degree of saturation:** When the soil is not fully saturated, the voids are partially occupied by air. The entrapped air blocks the passage of water and reduces permeability.
- **Impurities in water:** Any impure particle in water has the tendency to block the conduit of flow, and thus reducing the permeability.

3.1.3 Determination of Coefficient of Permeability

Coefficient of permeability can be determined using both laboratory and field tests. In the laboratory, different methods are used for the determination of coefficient of permeability of fine grained and coarse-grained soils.

3.1.3.1 Constant Head Permeability Test

The coefficient of permeability of a relatively more permeable soil (coarse grained) can be determined in laboratory by the constant head permeability test where a reasonable discharge can be collected in time interval (Fig. 3.1). The coefficient of permeability (k) is computed using the equation.

$$k = \frac{Q}{t} \cdot \frac{L}{h} \cdot \frac{1}{A} \tag{3.4}$$

where,

Q - the quantity of flow in a time interval t

L - length of the sample,

h - head causing flow,

A - Total cross-sectional area of the sample

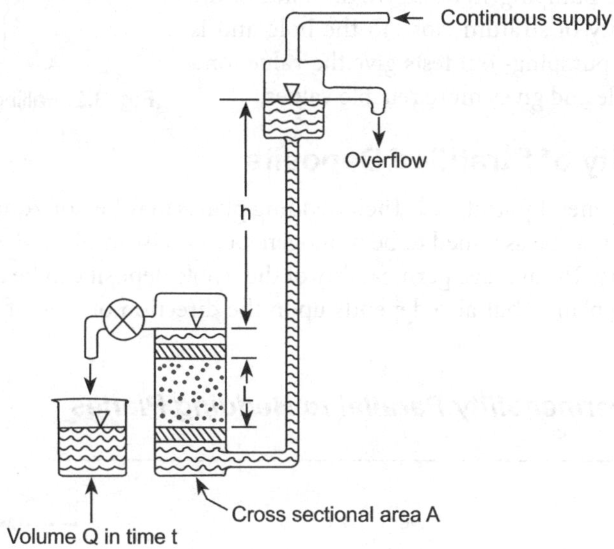

Fig. 3.1: Constant permeability test

3.1.3.2 Falling Head Permeability Test or Variable Head Permeability Test

For relatively less permeable soils (fine grained), the quantity of water collected in the graduated jar of the constant-head permeability test is very small and cannot be measured accurately (Fig 3.2). In case of such soils, the variable head permeability test is used. The value of k is computed using the equation,

$$k = 2.30 \frac{aL}{At} log_{10} \left(\frac{h_1}{h_2} \right) \tag{3.5}$$

where,

α - Cross-sectional area of the standpipe,

L - Length of the sample,

A - Total cross-sectional area of the sample,

h_1 - Head at time t_1,

h_2 - Head at time t_2,

$t = t_2 - t_1$, the time interval during which the head reduces from h_1 to h_2.

Preparing soil samples in laboratory with the same particle arrangement and density is very difficult and hence the results of field permeability tests are more suitable for practical applications. Field tests given in-situ values of permeability with minimum disturbance.

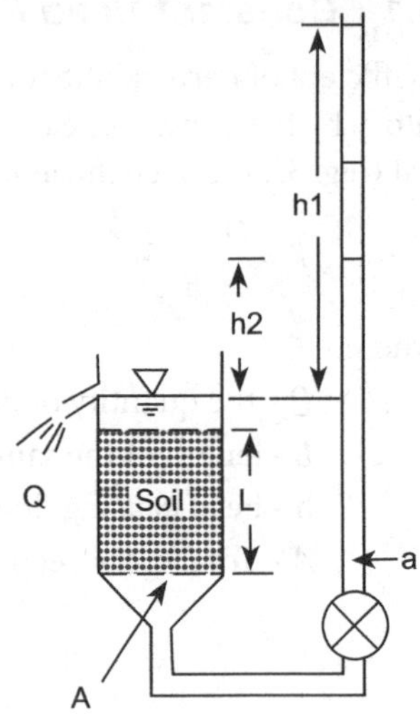

Fig. 3.2: Falling head permeability test

3.1.3.3 Field Tests

The field tests may be in the form of pumping out-tests or pumping- in tests wherein the water is pumped out or pumped into the drilled wells. The pumping-in tests give the value of the coefficient of permeability of stratum close to the hole and is economical whereas the pumping- out tests give the value for a large area around the hole and gives more reliable values.

3.1.4 Permeability of Stratified Deposits

Soil deposits in field are generally stratified. Their bedding planes may be horizontal, inclined or vertical. In such cases, each layer may be assumed to be homogeneous and isotropic and with a separate value of coefficient of permeability. The average permeability of the whole deposit can be calculated based on the direction of the bedding planes, but also depends upon the direction of flow of water through the soil mass.

3.1.4.1 Average Permeability Parallel to Bedding Planes

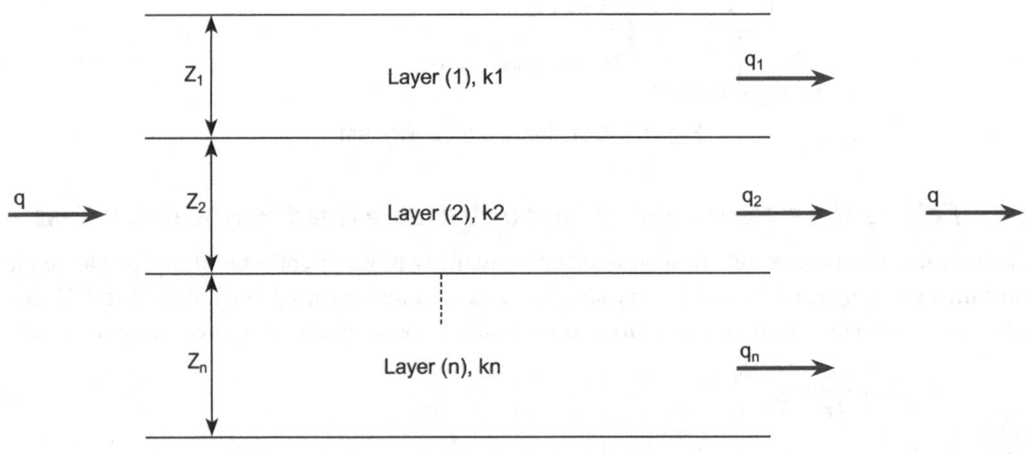

Fig. 3.3: Flow parallel to bedding planes

$$k_X = \frac{k_1 Z_1 + k_2 Z_2 + k_3 Z_3 + ... + k_n Z_n}{Z_1 + Z_2 + Z_3 ... + Z_n} \tag{3.6}$$

where,

k_X = Average permeability of the soil deposit parallel to the Bedding planes.

$Z_1 + Z_2 + Z_3 + \ldots + Z_n$ - Thickness of individual layers

$k_1, k_2, k_3, \ldots, k_n$ - Coefficient of permeability of the individual layers,

$q_1, q_2, q_3, \ldots, q_n$ - Discharge through the individual layers.

3.1.4.2 *Average Permeability Perpendicular to Bedding Planes*

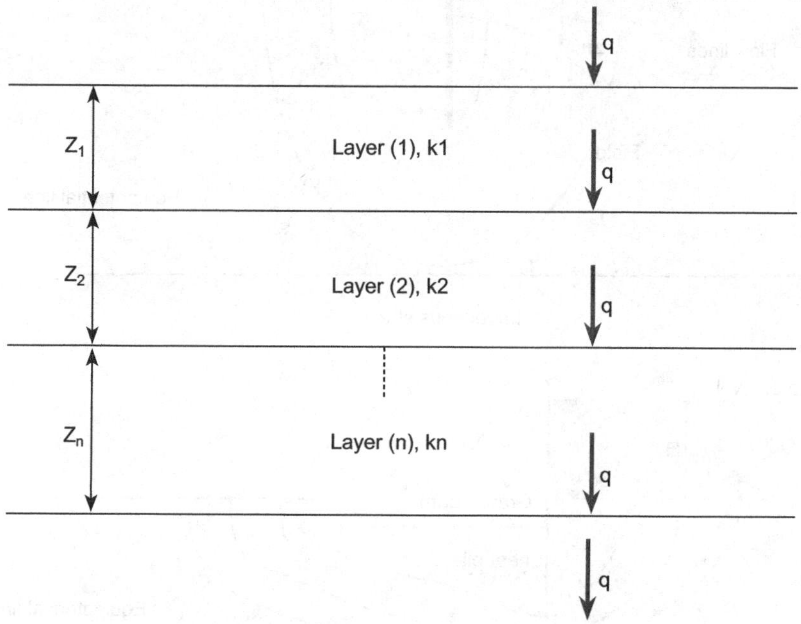

Fig. 3.4: Flow perpendicular to bedding planes

$$k_y = \frac{Z_1 + Z_2 + Z_3 + \ldots + Z_n}{\left(\frac{Z_1}{k_1}\right) + \left(\frac{Z_2}{k_2}\right) + \left(\frac{Z_3}{k_3}\right) + \ldots + \left(\frac{Z_n}{k_n}\right)} \tag{3.7}$$

where,

k_y - Average permeability of the soil deposit perpendicular to the bedding planes,

$Z_1 + Z_2 + Z_3 + \ldots + Z_n$ - Thickness of individual layers,

$i_1, i_2, i_3, \ldots, i_n$ - Hydraulic gradient for each stratum,

$k_1, k_2, k_3, \ldots, k_n$ - Coefficient of permeabilities of the individual layers.

3.1.5 Seepage Analysis

Seepage is the flow of water under gravitational forces through a permeable medium. The flow is generally laminar and takes place from a point of high head to a point of low head. During this process of seepage, the path that is followed by a water particle is marked as a flow line. The lines connect points of equal head on various flow lines are known as equipotential lines. Both these lines intersect each other at right angles, and a small area covered by a pair of flow lines and equipotential lines is called a field.

The flow lines and equipotential lines together form a flow net (Fig. 3.5) that provides a pictorial representation of the path taken by water particles and the pressure variation along the flow path.

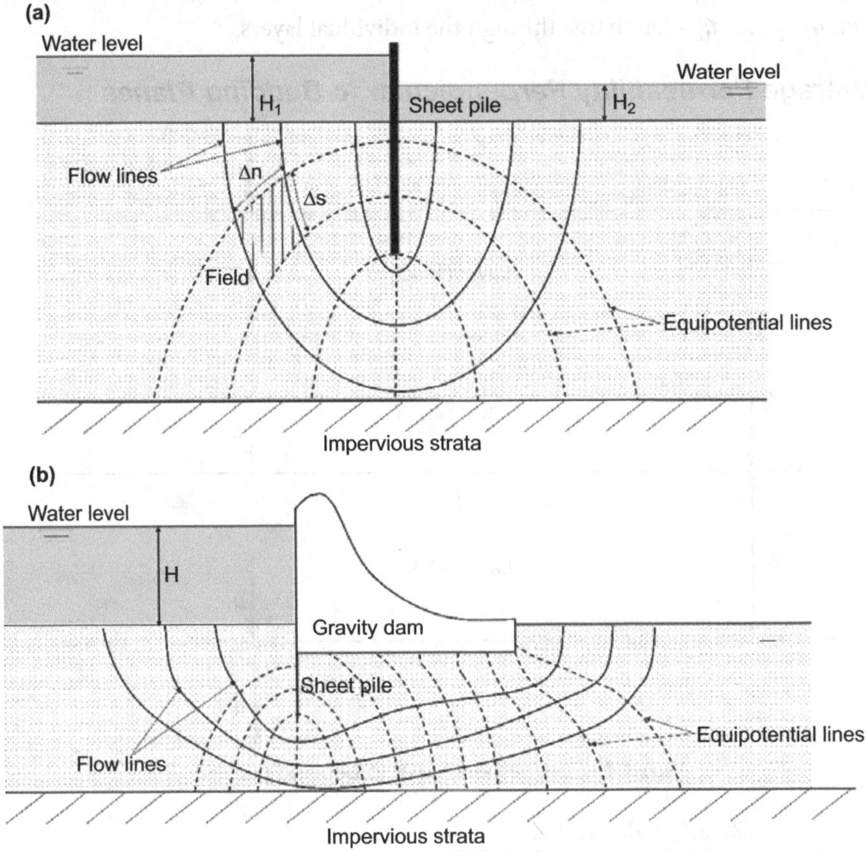

Fig. 3.5: Flow nets. (a) below a sheet pile, and (b) below a gravity dam

Flow nets are constructed with the following assumptions, using Laplace equation:

- The flow is two dimensional
- Water and soil are incompressible
- Soil is isotropic and homogeneous
- The soil is fully saturated
- The flow is steady
- Darcy's law is valid.

3.1.5.1 Properties of Flow Net

The properties of flow net can be summarized as under:

- Every intersection between a flow line and an equipotential line should be at right angles.
- The discharge (Δq) between any two adjacent flow lines is constant.

- The drop of head (Δh) between the two adjacent equipotential lines is constant.
- The ratio of the length and width of each field ($\Delta s/\Delta n$) is constant.
- Smaller the dimension of the field, greater will be the hydraulic gradient and velocity of flow through it.
- In a homogeneous soil, every transition in the shape of the curves is smooth, being either elliptical or parabolic in shape.

3.1.5.2 Applications or Uses of Flow Net

A flow net can be used for the following purposes:

- **Determination of seepage flow (Discharge)**

$$q = k.h.\frac{N_f}{N_d} \tag{3.8}$$

where,

q - Discharge through a flow net,
k - Coefficient of permeability,
h - Total hydraulic head causing flow,
N_f - Number of flow channels, and
N_d - Number of equipotential drops.

The above expression is valid for isotropic soils per unit length of structure perpendicular to the plane of section and should be multiplied by the length of structure to get the total discharge.

- **Determination of hydraulic gradient**

The average value of hydraulic gradient for any flow field is given by

$$i = \frac{\Delta h}{\Delta s} \tag{3.9}$$

where,

Δs - the length of flow field.

At the exit, the length Δs is minimum and the hydraulic gradient is generally maximum, and velocity is also maximum.

- **Determination of total head**

The total head (h) at any point (P) is given by

$$h_p = h - nx\frac{h}{N_d} \tag{3.10}$$

where,

n - the number of equipotential drops upto point P.

Hence, the seepage pressure at any point (P) is obtained by simply multiplying total head at P (h_p) with the unit weight of water (γ_w) and this pressure acts in the direction of flow.

- **Determination of pressure head**

The pressure head at any point is equal to the total head minus the elevation head. The downstream water level is generally (usually) taken as datum.

3.1.6 Seepage Pressure

As the water flows through a soil, it exerts a force on the soil. The force acts in the direction of Bow in the case of isotropic soils. The force is known as the drag force or seepage force. The pressure induced in the soil is termed seepage pressure.
The seepage force (J) is given by

$$J = \gamma_w hA \tag{3.11}$$

The seepage force per unit volume (j) is expressed as

$$j = \frac{\gamma_w hA}{AL} = \frac{h}{L}\gamma_w \tag{3.12}$$

The seepage pressure (p_s) is the seepage force per unit area.

$$p_s = \frac{J}{A} = \frac{\gamma_w hA}{A} \tag{3.13}$$

The seepage pressure (p_s) can be expressed in terms of the hydraulic gradient.

$$p_s = \gamma_w h = \gamma_w \frac{h}{L} L \tag{3.14}$$

$$p_s = i\gamma_w L \tag{3.15}$$

L - Length of the sample,

A - Cross-sectional area of the sample,

h - Hydraulic head,

γ_w – Unit weight of water.

3.1.7 Concept of Effective Stress

In a loaded soil mass which is below water, there are two types of stresses that act within soil mass: effective stress, and neutral stress or pore water pressure.

3.1.7.1 *Effective Stress*

It is also known as inter-granular pressure. It is transferred to soil grains through their point of contact of the interconnected particles of a soil and is represented by $\bar{\sigma}$ or σ'.

3.1.7.2 *Pore Water Pressure*

It is transmitted to the soil base through the pore water and is represented by u.

The effective stress cannot be measured directly in the laboratory. It is deduced from total stress and pore water pressure.

$$\bar{\sigma} \; or \; \sigma' = \sigma - u \tag{3.16}$$

where,

$\bar{\sigma} \; or \; \sigma'$ - effective stress,

σ - total stress,

u - pore water pressure.

In fully saturated condition, the vertical downward effective stress acting on soil of Z depth is $\gamma_{sub}Z$. When the upward seepage pressure becomes equal to this value, cohesionless soil losses its shear strength. This condition in saturated cohesionless soil is called quicksand condition or boiling condition. The critical gradient at quicksand condition is given by:

$$i_c = \frac{\gamma_{sub}}{\gamma_w} = \frac{G-1}{1+e} \tag{3.17}$$

where γ_{sub} is the submerged unit weight of soil, γ_w is the unit weight of water, G is the specific gravity of soil, and e is the void ratio of soil.

3.1.8 Seepage Velocity

The velocity of water through the pore spaces in fluid is called seepage velocity (V_s). This velocity is always greater than or equal to the discharge velocity, due to the reduction in cross sectional area. It can be calculated as follows:

$$V_s = \frac{V}{n} \tag{3.18}$$

where V is the discharge velocity and n is the porosity of soil.

3.1.9 Seepage Through Earthen Structures

When an earthen dam is constructed, water seeps through the dam body. For a homogenous earthen dam with an impervious foundation, the impermeable boundary is a flow line which forms the lower boundary of the flow net. The topmost flow line is known as phreatic line (Fig. 3.6) or seepage line, and the pressure acting on this line is equivalent to atmospheric pressure. The soil is unsaturated above the phreatic line and saturated below the phreatic line. As the pressure head is zero on the phreatic line, the total head is equal to the elevation head.

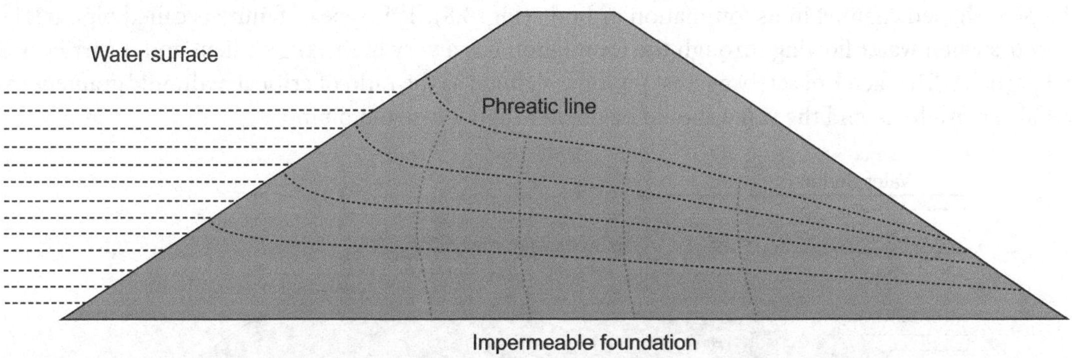

Fig. 3.6: Phreatic line through an earthen dam

Once the phreatic line has been located, the flow net can be drawn, and the discharge can be computed using the equation

$$q = k.h.\frac{N_f}{N_d} \tag{3.19}$$

It is also computed using the equation, $q = ks$

where,

s is the focal distance given by:

$$s = \sqrt{d^2 + h^2} - d$$

where

$$d = bottom\ width\ of\ the\ dam - length\ of\ the\ filter - 0.7\,b$$

where

$$b = n\,h$$

Upstream slope is given by 1: *n (V:H)* and h is the water depth.

If a provision for drainage is provided at the downstream side, the seepage path and thus the phreatic line of the dam will get modified as shown in Fig. 3.7.

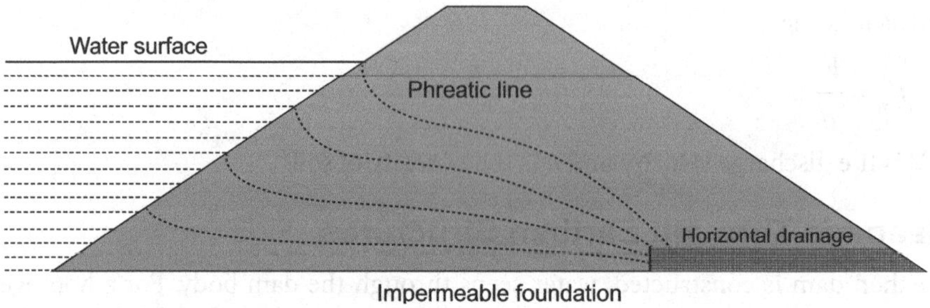

Fig. 3.7: Phreatic line through an earthen dam with horizontal filter

3.1.9.1 Piping

Hydraulic structures, such as weirs and dams, built on pervious foundations sometimes fail formation of a pipe-shaped channel in its foundation or body (Fig. 3.8). This type of failure is called piping failure. It occurs when water flowing through the foundation has a very high exit gradient and it carries with it soil particles. The factor of safety against piping is defined as the ratio of critical hydraulic gradient to the actual exit gradient, and the value should be greater than 4 to avoid piping.

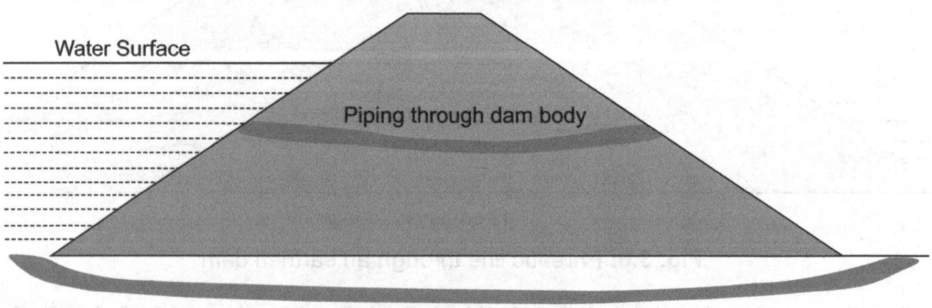

Fig. 3.8: Piping through dam body and foundation

The following measures are usually adopted to prevent piping failures.

- **Increasing the path of percolation**
  The length of the path of percolation can be increased by increasing the base width of the hydraulic structure, by providing vertical cut off walls below the hydraulic structure or by providing an upstream impervious blanket, as shown in Fig. 3. 9

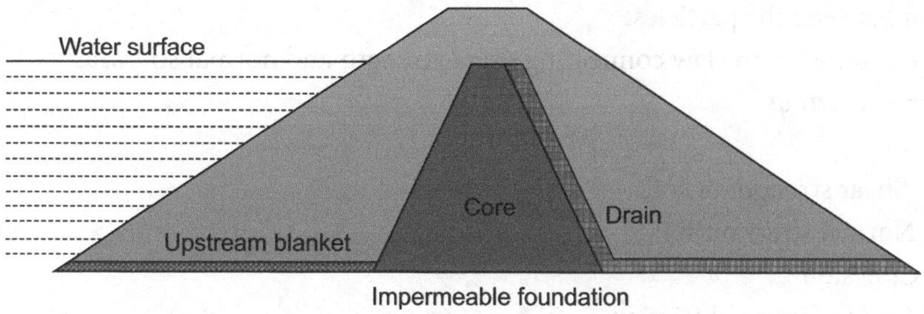

Fig. 3.9: Measures to control piping

- **Impervious core**
  The quantity of seepage is reduced by providing an impervious core (Fig. 3. 9).
- **Providing Drainage Filter or loaded filter**
  The drainage filter may be horizontal or in the form of a rock toe. It may also be in the form of a chimney drain, as shown in Fig. 3. 9. A loaded filter consists of coarse-grained particles such as sands and gravels. It is provided in order to increase the downward seepage force without a rise in the upward seepage force.

3.2 SHEAR STRENGTH OF SOIL

Shear strength of a soil is its maximum resistance to shear stresses just before the failure. Most engineering applications of soil, such as, stability of slopes, lateral pressure exerted by soil on retaining walls, and bearing capacity of soil requires knowledge of shear strength of soil.

3.2.1 Components of Shearing Resistance

Shearing resistance is composed of

(i) Cohesion, and

(ii) Friction,

Strength of cohesionless soils comes mostly from intergranular friction alone and cohesive soils from cohesion alone, while in other soils it comes from both cohesion and internal friction.

Cohesion is the force of attraction between the particles binding them together. Cohesion is present in clays and silts but is normally absent in sands and gravels. Internal friction is due to the inter-locking of particles. All soils except plastic undrained clay exhibit friction.

3.2.2 Classification of Soils

Based on cohesion and friction, soils can be classified into φ – soils, c- soils and $c - \varphi$ soils.

φ – soils are cohesion less or frictional or coarse-grained soils. e.g., sands and gravels. c- soils are called frictionless cohesive or fine-grained soils. e.g., clays. $c - \varphi$ soils are called cohesive and frictional soils like silts.

3.2.3 Mohr-Coulomb Failure Theory

Mohr stated that shear failure of any soil happens with a combination of both shear and normal stresses. He also stated that the shear stress on failure plane is a function f normal stress acting along that plane. Later, Coulomb separated the shear strength of soil into two components:

(i) Cohesion between the particles

(ii) Friction between the particles.

He proposed a straight-line law connecting shear strength and normal stress, as

$$\tau_f = c + \tan\varphi \tag{3.20}$$

where,

τ_f - Shear strength of soil,

σ - Normal stress on soil,

c - Cohesion

φ- Angle of internal friction.

The inclination of the failure envelope to the horizontal gives the angle of shearing resistance and its intercept on the vertical axis is equal to the cohesion. The equation of shear strength can be further simplified based on the type of soil as shown in Fig. 3. 10.

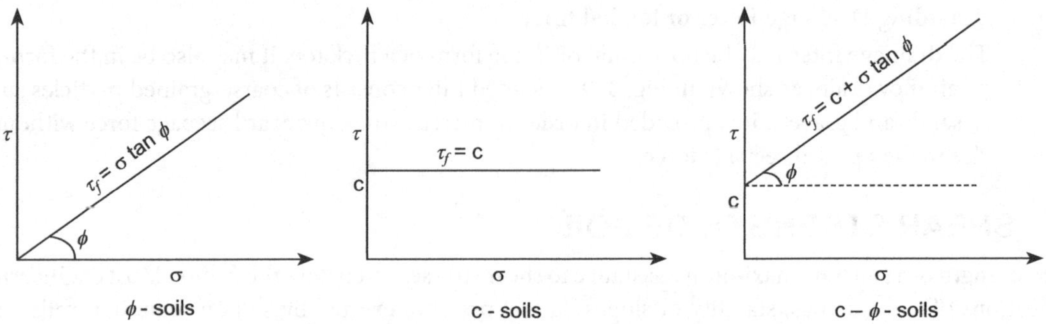

Fig. 3.10: Failure envelopes for different types of soil

3.2.4 Modified Mohr-Coulomb Failure Theory

Terzaghi established that the strength of soil is controlled by effective stresses and not by total stresses.

In terms of effective stresses, Eq. (3.19) is written as

$$\tau_f = c' + \bar{\sigma} \tan\varphi' \tag{3.21}$$

where,

$\bar{\sigma}$ - Effective normal stress $= \sigma - \mu$

σ - total normal stress.

u - Pore water pressure,

c' - cohesion in terms of effective stresses and

and φ' - angle of shearing resistance in terms of effective stresses.

3.2.5 Determination of Shear Strength

The shear test must be conducted under appropriate drainage conditions that simulate the actual field case.

In shear tests, there are two stages. In the first stage normal stress (or confining pressure) is applied to the specimen. Later, in the second stage shear stress (or deviator stress) is applied to the specimen to shear it.

Depending upon the drainage conditions, there are three types of tests: Unconsolidated- Undrained (UU) tests, Consolidated-Undrained (CU) tests and Consolidated-Drained (CD) tests. The shear force is applied either by increasing the shear displacement at a given rate or by increasing the shear force at a given rate. Accordingly, the shear tests, are called either strain controlled, or stress controlled.

The following tests are used to measure the shear strength of soil.

I. Direct shear test
II. Triaxial test
III. Unconfined compression test
IV. Vane shear test

3.2.5.1 Direct Shear Test

Direct shear test can be conducted for any one of the three drainage conditions. A number of identical specimens are tested under different normal stresses. The shear stress required to cause failure is determined for each normal stress. The failure envelope is obtained by plotting and joining the points corresponding to shear strength at different normal stresses by a straight line (Fig. 3.11).

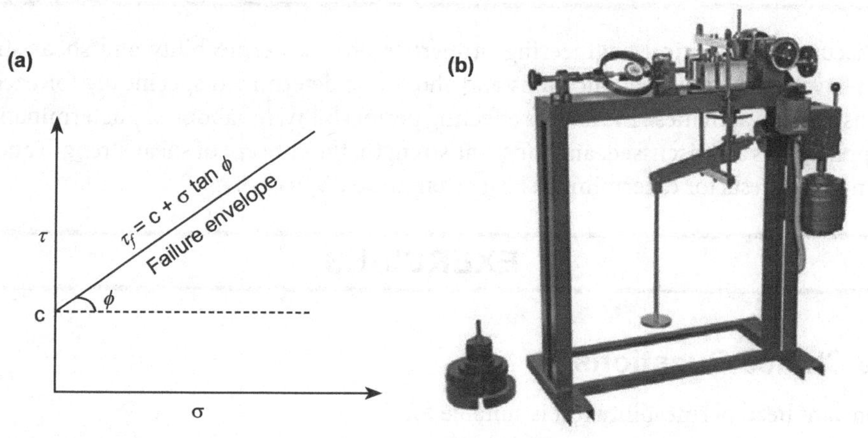

Fig. 3.11: Direct shear test. (a) Failure envelope and (b) laboratory test set up

3.2.5.2 Vane Shear Test

This is a quick test, used either in the field or in the laboratory, to determine the undrained shear strength of cohesive soils. A vane shear test apparatus has four steel plates fixed at right angles to each other to a steel rod (Fig. 3.12), and the vanes are pushed into soil and rotated at a constant speed (1 rpm). A calibrated torsion spring measures the resistance of soil to rotation, and the shear strength is determined by the following formula if both top and bottom end shear the soil.

$$\tau_f = \frac{T}{\Pi D^2\left[(H/2)+(D/6)\right]} \quad (3.22)$$

If only bottom end take part in shearing, then

$$\tau_f = \frac{T}{\Pi D^2\left[(H/2)+(D/12)\right]} \quad (3.23)$$

where

T - Maximum torque at failure.

H - Height of vanes,

D - Diameter of rotating blades.

The vane shear test can also be used to determine the sensitivity of the soil. After the initial test, the vane is rotated rapidly through several revolutions. The test is then caried out on the remoulded soil and the shear strength in remoulded state is determined.

Thus,

$$Sensitivity(S_t) = \frac{(\tau_f)_{(undistributed)}}{(\tau_f)_{(remoulded)}} \quad (3.24)$$

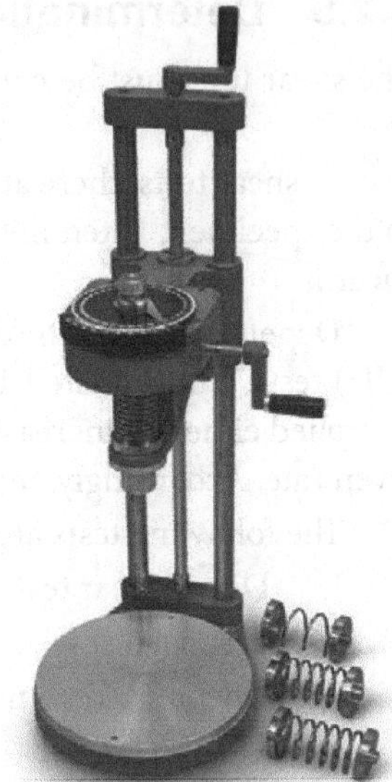

Fig. 3.12: Laboratory vane shear test setup

UNIT SUMMARY

The unit discusses two critical engineering properties of soil, permeability and shear strength. Both are highly relevant in practical applications and should be determined specifically for each site, before starting construction activities. The factors affecting permeability, its laboratory determination and some practical applications are discussed, and for shear strength, the concept of shear strength and direct shear test and vane shear tests for determining shear strength ae discussed.

EXERCISES

Multiple Choice Questions

1. Constant head permeability test is suitable for:
   (a) Granular soils
   (b) Fine-grained soils
   (c) Cohesive soils
   (d) All the above
2. Which among the following is not an assumption while constructing flow nets?
   (a) The flow is two dimensional
   (b) Water and soil are incompressible
   (c) Soil is isotropic and homogeneous
   (d) The soil is partially saturated

3. Effective stress in soil is defined as the difference between total stress and ....
   (a) Normal stress (b) Shear stress
   (c) Pore water pressure (d) None of the above
4. Which among the following is not a widely followed shear test condition, based on drainage?
   (a) Unconsolidated-Undrained (UU) tests,
   (b) Consolidated-Undrained (CU) tests
   (c) Unconsolidated-Drained (UD) tests
   (d) Consolidated-Drained (CD) tests.

Answers of Multiple Choice Questions			
1. (a)	2. (d)	3. (c)	4. (c)

Numerical

Examples:

1. A 20 cm long, 8 cm diameter coarse sand sample was tested in a constant head permeability test. After 15 mins of constant water flow under 1 m head, the volume of discharged water was found to be 1200 cc. Calculate the coefficient of permeability of soil.

$$t = 15\,\text{min} = 900\,sec$$

$$h = 1m = 100\,cm$$

$$A = \frac{\pi}{4}d^2 = \frac{\pi}{4}8^2 = 50.26\,cm^2$$

$$L = 20\,cm$$

$$Q = 1200\,cm^3$$

$$k = \frac{QL}{thA} = \frac{1200\times 20}{900\times 100\times 50.26} = 5.306\times 10^{-3}\,cm/s$$

2. The water level in a standpipe of 6 mm diameter reduced from 80 cm to 25 cm in a duration of 15 mins in a variable head permeability test. The soil sample had a height of 12 cm and a cross sectional area of 44.41 cm^2. Find the coefficient of permeability.

$$a = \frac{\pi}{4}d^2 = \frac{\pi}{4}0.6^2 = 0.28\,cm^2$$

$$L = 12\,cm$$

$$A = 44.41\,cm^2$$

$$h_1 = 80\,cm$$

$$h_2 = 25\,cm$$

$$t = 15\,\text{min} = 900\,s$$

$$k = 2.30\frac{aL}{At}log_{10}\left(\frac{h_1}{h_2}\right)$$

$$= 2.30\frac{0.28\times12}{44.41\times900}log_{10}\left(\frac{80}{25}\right)$$

$$=9.86\times10^{-5}\ cm/s$$

3. A silty sand soil has a cohesion of 25 kPa and an angle of internal friction of 25°. Calculate the shear strength of the soil at 5 m below the ground surface, is the unit weight of soil in 18 kN/m³ and water table is well below the layer of soil.

$$c = 25\,kPa$$

$$\varphi = 25^o$$

$$\sigma = \gamma Z = 18\times5 = 90\,kPa$$

$$\tau_f = c + \sigma tan\varphi$$

$$= 25 + 90\times\tan(25)$$

$$= 66.97\,kPa$$

4. A soil sample with cohesion 20kPa was tested using a direct shear test with an applied normal stress of 200kPa. The sample failed at a shear stress of 150 kPa. Calculate the angle of internal friction of soil.

$$c = 20\,kPa$$

$$\sigma = 200\,kPa$$

$$\tau_f = 150\,kPa = c + \sigma tan\varphi$$

$$\Phi = \tan^{-1}\left(\frac{\tau_f - c}{\sigma}\right)$$

$$= \tan^{-1}\left(\frac{150-20}{200}\right) = 33.02^o$$

Exercises

1. A stratified soil deposit has 3 layers of soil. The top layer consists of 2 m deep soil with coefficient of permeability 5×10^{-4} cm/s and the second layer is 5 m thick and more permeable, with coefficient of permeability 2×10^{-2} cm/s. These layers are overlaid on top of a 2 m thick layer of coefficient of permeability 3×10^{-3} cm/s. Calculate the average coefficient of permeability in directions parallel to the bedding and perpendicular to the bedding.

$k_h = 1.1\times10^{-2}\ cm/s$, $k_v = 1.9\times10^{-3}\ cm/s$

2. The following are the observations from a direct shear test, during failure. Calculate the cohesion and angle of internal friction of the soil sample from the observations.

$c = 10\ kPa$ and $\varphi = 30°$

Sample No.	Normal stress (kPa)	Shear stress (kPa)
1	20	21.55
2	40	33.09

Sample No.	Normal stress (kPa)	Shear stress (kPa)
3	60	44.64

3. A soil sample has been taken from a uniform deposit of dry sand and the unit weight was found to be 19 kN/m^3 and angle of internal friction was found to be 35°. Calculate the shear strength of the soil on a horizontal plane, at 4m depth from the surface.

$$\tau_f = 53.2\ kPa$$

4. A structure is proposed on the site mentioned in question 3, which will induce 60 kN/m^2 stress in the vertical direction and 70 kN/m^2 stress in the horizontal direction at 4 m depth. Will the increase in shear stress exceed the shear strength of soil on horizontal plane?

$$\tau_f = 95.2\ kPa,\ hence\ stable$$

5. At a depth of 6 m below the ground surface at a site, a vane shear test gave a torque value of 6500 N-cm. The vane was 10 cm high and 6 cm across the blades. What will be the shear strength of the soil (in kN/m^2)?

$$\tau_f = 95.8\ kN/m^2$$

Short and Long Answer Type Questions

1. Define permeability.
2. What is Darcy's law? What is its significance in soil mechanics?
3. Enlist any two field tests carried out to determine the coefficient of permeability of soil.
4. What is effective stress in soil?
5. Explain Mohr-Coulomb failure theory.
6. Define effective size of particle in sieve analysis.
7. Explain in detail the procedure of constant head permeability test.
8. What are flow nets? What are the characteristics of flow nets?
9. What are the different measures adopted to control seepage through earthen dams?
10. Enlist and explain any two laboratory tests used to determine the shear strength of soil.

PRACTICALS

Name of experiment: Determination of coefficient of permeability by constant head method (IS 2720)

Aim: To determine the coefficient of permeability of the given soil sample by constant head method

Apparatus required: Permeameter mould with detachable base, drainage bade and drainage cap compacting equipment, constant head tank, graduated glass cylinder to receive the discharge, stop watch to note the time and a meter scale to measure the head differences and length of specimen.

Theory: Permeability is the property of a soil which allows the flow of water (or any other fluid) through its interconnecting pores. Determination of permeability is critical in solving number of engineering problems, settlements in foundations, yield of wells, and seepage through and below the earthen structures. When the soil is highly permeable, constant head permeability test is used to determine the coefficient f permeability.

Procedure:

1. Prepare the soil sample with the required degree of compaction.
2. Measure precisely the dimensions of soil sample.
3. For the constant head arrangement, the specimen shall be connected through the top inlet to the constant head reservoir.
4. Open the bottom outlet of the reservoir.
5. Wait till the flow of water becomes steady and note the head of water.
6. The quantity of flow for a convenient time interval may be collected.
7. Repeat step 6 two more times for the same interval.

Observations:

Experiment No.	1	2	3
Length of soil sample L (cm)			
Area of soil sample A (cm^2)			
Time t (s)			
Quantity of water collected Q (cm^3)			
Head of water h (cm)			
Coefficient of permeability k (cm/s) $k = \frac{QL}{thA}$			

Result:

Inference:

Name of experiment: Determination of coefficient of permeability by falling head method (IS 2720)

Aim: To determine the coefficient of permeability of the given soil sample by falling head method

Apparatus required: Permeameter with its accessories, weighing balance of 1 gm sensitivity, stopwatch, measuring jar, meter scale, water container.

Theory: Permeability is the property of a soil which allows the flow of water (or any other fluid) through its interconnecting pores. Determination of permeability is critical in solving number of engineering problems, settlements in foundations, yield of wells, and seepage through and below the earthen structures. The falling head test is suited for soil with low discharge, like clays and silts.

Procedure:

1. Prepare the soil specimen as specified and saturate the specimen.
2. Assemble the permeameter in the bottom tank and fill the tank with water.
3. Connect the nozzle to the standpipe. Wait until steady flow is obtained.

4. Note down the time interval t for a fall of head in the standpipe h.
5. Repeat step 4 two more times to determine t for the same head.

Observations:

Experiment No.	1	2	3
Area of standpipe a, cm^2 Cross sectional area of soil specimen A, cm^2 Length of soil specimen, L, cm Initial reading of standpipe, h_1, cm Final reading of standpipe, h_2, cm Time, t, s Coefficient of permeability, k, cm/s			
$k = 2.30\frac{aL}{At}\log_{10}\left(\frac{h_1}{h_2}\right)$			

Result:

Inference:

Name of experiment: Determination of shear strength of soil using direct shear test (IS 2720)

Aim: To determine the shear strength of the given soil sample using direct shear test

Apparatus required: Direct shear box apparatus, dial gauge, proving ring, weighing balance.

Theory: Shear strength of a soil is its maximum resistance to shear stresses just before the failure. Most engineering applications of soil, such as, stability of slopes, lateral pressure exerted by soil on retaining walls, and bearing capacity of soil requires knowledge of the value of the angle of internal friction and cohesion of the soil, which are the shear strength parameters.

Procedure:

1. Check the inner dimension of the soil container.
2. Place the soil in smooth layers and tamp the soil to achieve the required density.
3. Measure the thickness of soil specimen.
4. Apply the desired normal load.
5. Remove the shear pin.
6. Attach the proving ring
7. Before proceeding to test check all adjustments to see that there is no connection between two parts except sand/soil.

8. Start the motor. Take the reading of the shear load at failure
9. Add an equal increment of normal stress and continue the experiment till failure
10. Record carefully all the readings. Set the dial gauges zero, before starting the experiment

Observations:

Experiment No.	1	2	3
Cross sectional area of specimen (cm^2)			
Normal load (kg)			
Normal stress (kPa) (Normal load/ cross sectional area)			
Shear load at failure (kg)			
Shear stress at failure (kPa) (Shear load / cross sectional area)			

Result:

Inference:

Name of experiment: Determination of shear strength of soil using vane shear test (IS 2720) **Aim:** To determine the shear strength of the given soil sample using vane shear test **Apparatus required:** Vane shear apparatus, container for soil specimen, callipers.

Theory: Shear strength of a soil is its maximum resistance to shear stresses just before the failure. Vane shear test is a quick method for determining shear strength. The laboratory vane shear test for the measurement of undrained strength of cohesive soils, and soils of low shear strength.

Procedure:

1. Prepare three specimens of the soil sample of dimensions of at least 37.5 mm diameter, with L/D ratio 2 or 3.
2. Mount the specimen container with the specimen on the base of the vane shear apparatus.
3. Gently lower the shear vanes into the specimen to their full length without disturbing the soil specimen.
4. Note the readings of the angle of twist.
5. Rotate the vanes at an uniform rate until the specimen fails.
6. Note the final reading of the angle of twist.
7. Find the value of blade height in cm.
8. Find the value of blade width in cm.

Observations:

Height of blade, H, cm =

Width of blade, D, cm =

Experiment No.			
Initial Reading (Deg)			
Final Reading (Deg.)			
Difference (Deg.)			
Spring Constant, kg-cm			
Torque, T = Spring Constant/180 × Difference, kg-cm			
Shear strength, $\tau_f = \frac{T}{\Pi D^2\left[(H/2)+(D/6)\right]}$, kg/cm^2			
Average shear strength, kg/cm^2			

Result:

Inference:

KNOW MORE

Teton Dam was an earth fill dam across the Teton River in Madison County located in south- eastern Idaho. The dam and its reservoir were the principal elements of the Teton Basin Project. The 93 m (305 ft.) high dam with a crest length of 975 m (3200 ft), failed completely during first filling on 5th June 1976. On June 3, 1976, two small seeps were observed at the downstream toe of the dam. The rest of the dam was inspected, and no further evidence of seepage was noted. Only two days later, the seepage became muddy, and a sinkhole developed on the downstream slope of the embankment dam. The structure was breached because of internal seepage, causing the loss of 11 lives and extensive flooding in the farmland and towns below the dam.

REFERENCES AND SUGGESTED READINGS

- Arora,K.R., "Soil Mechanics and Foundation Engineering," Standard Publishers Distributors, Delhi, 2008.
- Gulhati, S. K.; Datta, M." Geotechnical engineering, Tata McGraw-Hill, New Delhi, 2005.

- IS 2720 (Part XVII) – 1986 (Reaffirmed 2002): Methods of test for soils, Part XVII Laboratory determination of permeability.
- IS 2720 (Part XIII) – 1986 (Reaffirmed 2002): Methods of test for soils, Part XIII Direct shear test
- IS:2720 (Part XXX)-1980 (Reaffirmed 2007): Methods of test for soils, Part XXX Laboratory vane shear test

Dynamic QR Code for Further Reading

4 Bearing Capacity of Soil

UNIT SPECIFICS

Through this unit we shall discuss the following aspects:

- Concept of bearing capacity
- Terzaghi's bearing capacity theory
- Field methods for determination of bearing capacity
- Definition of earth pressure
- Rankine's theory for non-cohesive soils

RATIONALE

This unit on the bearing capacity of soil deals with two important concepts in soil mechanics, the bearing capacity and lateral earth pressure. It speaks about both the vertical stress that a foundation can withstand without failure, and the lateral stress exerted by earth on a retaining wall. The unit deals with the application of concepts learnt in the previous units. Both foundations and retaining walls are important geotechnical structures, and this chapter deals with the theories related to the functioning of both.

PRE-REQUISITES

Basic concepts of soil mechanics.

UNIT OUTCOMES

List of outcomes of this unit is as follows:

U4-O1: Understand the concept of bearing capacity and the related terms.

U4-O2: Learn Terzaghi's theory of bearing capacity and the effect of water table in bearing capacity calculation.

U4-O3: Understand the field methods for testing bearing capacity.

U4-O4: Understand the concept of lateral earth pressure.

U4-O5: Learn Rankine's earth pressure theory for cohesionless soils.

Unit-4 Outcomes	EXPECTED MAPPING WITH COURSE OUTCOMES (1- Weak Correlation; 2- Medium correlation; 3- Strong Correlation)				
	CO-1	CO-2	CO-3	CO-4	CO-5
U4-O1	-	-	2	3	-
U4-O2	-	-	2	3	-
U4-O3	-	-	2	3	-
U4-O4	-	-	2	3	-
U4-O5	-	-	2	3	-

4.1 BEARING CAPACITY OF SOIL

The ultimate load of any structure is transferred to the soil through the foundations. Based the depth and width of foundations, they are primarily classified into shallow and deep foundations. The term bearing capacity is widely used in associated with shallow foundations, which are laid at a depth less than on equal to their widths. Shallow foundations are of different types; like isolated, strip and combined foundations. In this unit, we are discussing the bearing capacity theories related to strip foundations, that are used to provide a continuous, level strip of support to a linear structure such as a wall. The foundation transmits the load from superstructure to a larger area, and it should be designed in such a way that the settlements are always within the permissible limit, and the soil does not fail in shear. Bearing capacity is a term used to define the pressure that can be taken by the soil safely, without failure. There are different terminologies associated with the definition of bearing capacity.

4.1.1 Basic Definitions

4.1.1.1 Ultimate Bearing Capacity (q_u)

Ultimate bearing capacity denotes the total pressure at the base of foundation at which shear failure occurs in soil.

4.1.1.2 Net Ultimate Bearing Capacity (q_{nu})

It is the net increase in pressure due to the superstructure, at the base of foundation that leads to the shear failure of soil. It is the difference of ultimate bearing capacity and the overburden stress due to the soil above the base of foundation.

$$q_{nu} = q_u - \gamma D_f \tag{4.1}$$

where γ is the unit weight of soil and D_f is the depth of foundation. The product γD_f is the overburden pressure, which exists at the level of base of foundation, even before construction.

4.1.1.3 Net Safe Bearing Capacity (q_{ns})

It is the net pressure on soil that can be safely applied to the soil, without causing shear failure. This is calculated by considering a suitable factor of safety (*FS*), which is usually taken as 3.

$$q_{ns} = \frac{q_{nu}}{FS} \quad (4.2)$$

4.1.1.4 Gross Safe Bearing Capacity (q_s)

It is the gross pressure that the soil can withstand, without shear failure. The value is obtained by adding the overburden stress to the net safe bearing capacity.

$$q_s = q_{ns} + \gamma D_f \quad (4.3)$$

4.1.1.5 Net Safe Settlement Pressure (q_{np})

It is the net pressure that can be taken by the soil without exceeding the permissible settlement limits. The maximum allowable settlement depends upon the type of foundation.

4.1.1.6 Net Allowable Bearing Pressure (q_{na})

It is the net bearing pressure used for design of foundations. As the soil should satisfy both shear failure and settlement criteria, the net allowable bearing pressure is the smaller of net safe bearing capacity and the net safe settlement pressure. This value is also known as the allowable soil pressure or allowable bearing capacity.

4.1.2 Terzaghi's Bearing Capacity Theory

The bearing capacity theory proposed by Terzaghi in 1943 deals with strip footings, with the following assumptions:

- The base of footing is rough.
- The footing is laid at a shallow depth (less than or equal to the width).
- Shear strength of the soil above the base of footing is neglected.
- The loading of the footing is vertical and is uniformly distributed.
- Footing is long (L/B ratio is infinite, where L is the length and B is the breadth of the footing).
- The shear strength of soil is governed by Mohr-Coulomb criteria
- The ultimate bearing capacity of a strip footing of width B placed at a depth D_f is given by the Terzaghi's equation as follows:

$$q_u = c'N_c + \gamma D_f N_q + 0.5B\gamma N_\gamma \quad (4.4)$$

where, c' is the cohesion of the soil, γ is the unit weight and N_c , N_q and N_γ are dimensionless numbers, known as Terzaghi's bearing capacity factors. These numbers depend upon the angle of internal friction of the soil, and the values are tabulated in Table 4.1.

Table 4.1: Terzaghi's bearing capacity factors

φ'	General shear failure			Local shear failure		
	N_c	N_q	N_γ	N_c'	N_q'	N_γ'
0	5.7	1.0	0.0	5.7	1.0	0.0
5	7.3	1.6	0.5	6.7	1.4	0.2
10	9.6	2.7	1.2	8.0	1.9	0.5

φ_r	General shear failure			Local shear failure		
	N_c	N_q	N_γ	N_c'	N_q'	N_γ'
15	12.9	4.4	2.5	9.7	2.7	0.9
20	17.7	7.4	5.0	11.8	3.9	1.7
25	25.1	12.7	9.7	14.8	5.6	3.2
30	37.2	22.5	19.7	19.0	8.3	5.7
35	57.8	41.4	42.4	25.2	12.6	10.1
40	95.7	81.3	100.4	34.9	20.5	18.8
45	172.3	173.3	297.5	51.2	35.1	37.7
50	347.5	415.1	1153.2	81.3	65.6	87.1

The value of bearing capacity factors also depends upon the type of shear failure. The shear failures are classified into three by Vesic (1973) as general shear failure, local shear failure and punching shear failure.

4.1.2.1 General Shear Failure

During general shear failure, the settlement below the footing increases suddenly at a stress of q_u, and the failure extend to the ground surface (Fig. 4.1a). The failure always occurs with heave on both sides and occurs commonly in stiff clays and dense sands.

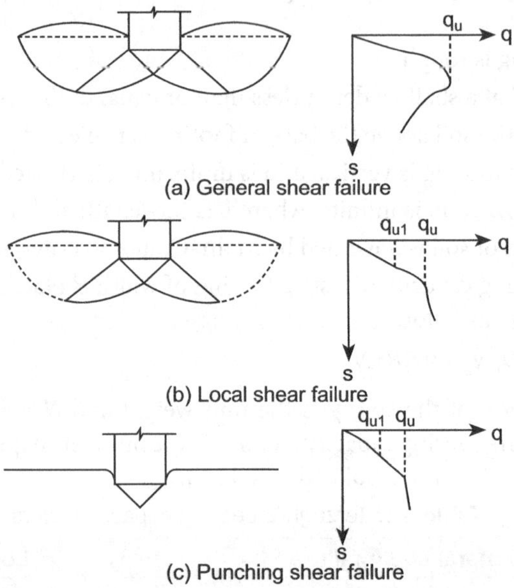

Fig. 4.1: Types of shear failure

4.1.2.2 Local Shear Failure

As can be observed in the load per unit area (q) vs settlement (s) curve in Fig. 4.1b, the movement starts at a load of q_{u1}, with sudden jerks in soil, and it gradually extends away from the foundation. For the failure surfaces to extend till the ground level, considerable movement is required. The load at this point is denoted as q_u, and when the load is exceeded beyond this, there is a substantial increase in settlement. Heaves are observed during local shear failure during large settlements. Local shear failure is commonly observed in medium dense sands and clays with medium consistency.

4.1.2.3 Punching Shear Failure

In the case of loose ands and soft clays, failure does not extend upto the ground surface. The jerk in foundation starts at a load of q_{u1} and the failure occurs at q_u. Beyond q_u, the load settlement curve is linear, and such failures are called punching shear failures. No heave is observed in this case.

4.1.3 Effect of Water Table on Bearing Capacity

Equation 4.4 for ultimate bearing capacity assumes that the water table is at great depth, and it has no effect on the bearing capacity of the foundation. The effect of water table is considered when it occurs at a depth between the ground level and a depth of $D_f + B$. In between these depths, two different conditions are considered as shown in Fig. 4.2. Any variation water table between ground level and base of footing will have effects on both second and third terms in the right-hand side of Eq. 4.4, and if water table is located below the base of footing but above a depth of $D_f + B$, only the last term will be affected.

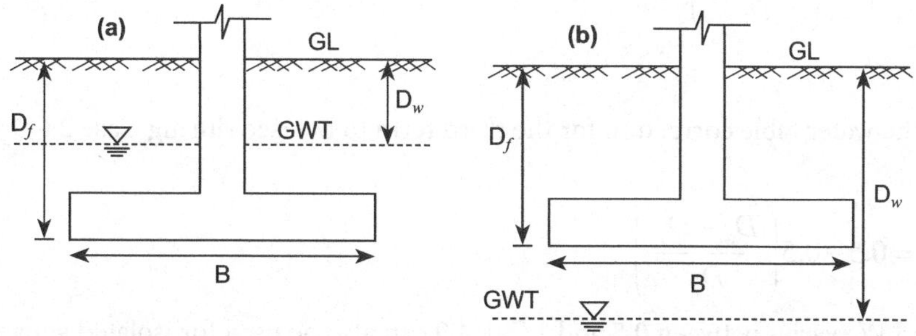

Fig. 4.2: Depth of water table below foundation (a) Case 1 and (b) Case II

4.1.3.1 Condition 1: Water Table Located Above the Base of Footing

The soil below the water table is in submerged condition, and the second term in Eq. 4.4 should be expressed in two parts. The first part considers the bulk unit weight of soil from ground surface to the depth of water table (D_w), and the second part considering submerged unit weight (γ') from the level of water table to the base of footing as shown in Eq. 4.5. The unit weight to be considered in the terms in the right-hand side of Eq. 4.4. is also the submerged unit weight.

$$\gamma D_f = \gamma D_w + \gamma'\left(D_f - D_w\right) \tag{4.5}$$

Thus Eq. 4.4 gets modified as:

$$q_u = c'N_c + \left[\gamma D_w + \gamma'\left(D_f - D_w\right)\right]N_q + 0.5B\gamma' N_\gamma \tag{4.6}$$

4.1.3.2 Condition 2: Water Table Located Below the Base of Footing

In this case, the second term is not affected. The third term in the right-hand side of Eq. 4.4 gets modified into two parts, considering the submerged unit weight of soil below the water table.

$$B\gamma = \gamma(D_w - D_f) + \gamma'(D_f + B - D_w) \tag{4.7}$$

Eq. 4.4 is modified in this case as:

$$q_u = c'N_c + \gamma D_f N_q + 0.5[\gamma(D_w - D_f) + \gamma'(D_f + B - D_w)]N_\gamma \tag{4.8}$$

4.1.3.3 General Expression

If $D_w = D_f$, i.e., if the water table is at the base of footing, Eq. 4.6 is same as Eq. 4.4, and if $D_w = D_f + B$, Eq. 4.8 is same as Eq. 4.4. Considering the variation along the depth is linear, two correction factors can be added to the second and third terms in the right-hand side of Eq. 4.4, to formulate a general expression given by:

$$q_u = c'N_c + \gamma D_f N_q W_q + 0.5B\gamma N_\gamma W_\gamma \tag{4.9}$$

where W_q is the water table correction for the second term to be used in Case 1 ($D_f \geq D_w$), given by:

$$W_q = 1 - 0.5\left(\frac{D_f - D_w}{D_f}\right) \tag{4.10}$$

$$W_\gamma = 0.5$$

and W_γ is the water table correction for the third term to be used during Case 2 ($D_w \geq D_f$), given by:

$$W_\gamma = 0.5 + 0.5\left(\frac{D_w - D_f}{D_f}\right) \tag{4.11}$$

Both W_q and W_γ varies between 0.5 and 1. Eq. 4.9 can also be used for isolated square and circular footings with minor modifications. In both the cases, the first term on right hand side of Eq. 4.9 gets multiplied by 1.2. In case of square footing, the third term gets multiplied by 0.4, while the coefficient for third term is 0.3 in the case of circular footings. The term B represents width of square footing and diameter in the case of circular footings.

4.1.4 Settlement of Foundation

The allowable bearing pressure is decided based on both safe bearing capacity and settlement. The settlement in soil due to the external load should also be considered before deciding the dimensions for design. There are other causes also that may result in settlement, like underground erosion, landslides, frost and heave and vibrations, and if detected, suitable measures should be adopted to minimise these settlements as well.

The foundation settlement due to external loads has three different phases:

- **Immediate or elastic settlement** (S_i): This occurs during or immediately after the construction of the structure. It is also known as the distortion settlement as it is due to distortions caused by the external load.
- **Consolidation settlement** (S_c): This settlement occurs due to gradual expulsion of water from the voids of the soil and is determined using Terzaghi's theory of consolidation (see Unit 5).

- **Secondary Consolidation Settlement (S_s):** This settlement occurs after completion of the primary consolidation. The amount of settlement in this case is very minor and is usually ignored.

The total settlement (S) is given by:

$$S = S_i + S_c + S_s \tag{4.12}$$

IS 1904 -1986 gives the safe values for maximum and differential settlements for different types of foundation, as listed in Table 4. 2.

Table 4.2: Maximum and differential settlements (IS 1904 -1986)

	Sand and hard clay			Plastic clay		
	Max - Settlement	Diff - settlement	Angular Distortion	Max - settlement	Diff - settlement	Angular Distortion
(a) Isolated foundation						
(i) Steel structures	50 mm	0.0033 L	1/300	50 mm	0.0033 L	1/300
(ii) RCC structures	50 mm	0.0015 L	1/666	75 mm	0.0015 L	1/666
(b) Raft foundations						
(i) Steel structures	75 mm	0.0033 L	1/300	100 mm	0.0033 L	1/300
(ii) RCC structures	75 mm	0.002 L	1/500	100 mm	0.002 L	1/500

4.1.5 Field Methods for Determination of Bearing Capacity

IS 1904-1986 suggests that the safe bearing capacity of foundation should be calculated on the basis of field soil investigation results. For determining bearing capacity, plate load test is conducted in field as per IS 1888-1982.

4.1.5.1 Plate Load Test

To conduct a plate load test, the location should be selected based on the results of boring. Otherwise, it can also be conducted at an elevation of the proposed foundation in the worst estimated condition. If the depth of water table is within a depth equal to the width of the plate (B_P), the test shall be conducted at the level of water table. If water table is above the test level, it should be lowered to the test level by means of pumping out. The test pits are usually excavated with a width five times B_P, the size of the plate, to a depth equal to the depth of foundation (D_f). The test plate is usually a square of width varying from 300 mm to 750 mm, made of steel and is 25 mm thick. Occasionally, circular plates are also used. The dead load of all equipments including ball and socket, loading column, jack and steel plates should be noted before starting the test.

A central hole of the size $B_P \times B$, is excavated in the pit. The depth of the central hole (D_P) is obtained from the following relation:

$$\frac{D_P}{B_P} = \frac{D_f}{B_f} \tag{4.13}$$

where B_f is the width of foundation, and therefore,

$$D_P = (B_P/B_f) \times D_f \quad (4.14)$$

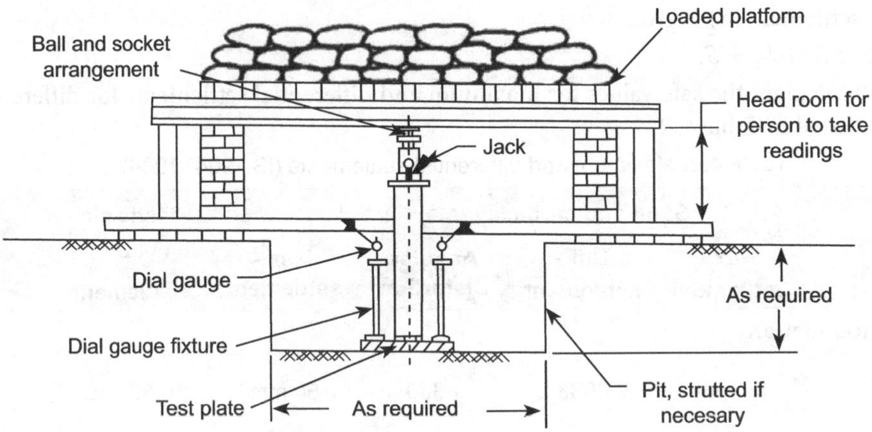

Fig. 4.3: Typical setup for plate load test

For conducting the plate load test, the plate is placed in the central hole and the load is applied by means of a hydraulic jack (Fig. 4. 3). Sometimes, trusses and reaction beam s are used instead of a loaded platform to take up the reaction. Wo dial gauges are required so that the settlement can be measured without any resetting in between. A seating load is first applied and released after some time. The load is then applied in increments of 1 kg/cm^2 or about 20% of the estimated ultimate bearing capacity, whichever is less. The settlement is recorded after 1, 2.25, 4, 6.25, 9, 16 and 25 minutes, and further at an interval of one hour to the nearest 0.02 mm. These hourly observations are continued for clayey soils until the rate of settlement is less than 0.2 mm/h. The test is conducted till twice the estimated design pressure or until failure or at least until the settlement of about 25 mm has occurred.

The ultimate load for the plate $q(p)$ is indicated by a break on the log-log plot between the load per unit area q and the settlement s. If the break is not well-defined, the ultimate load is taken as that corresponding to a settlement of one-fifth of the plate width (B_P). On the natural plot (Fig. 4.4), $q(p)$ is obtained from the intersection of the tangents drawn on load-settlement curve.

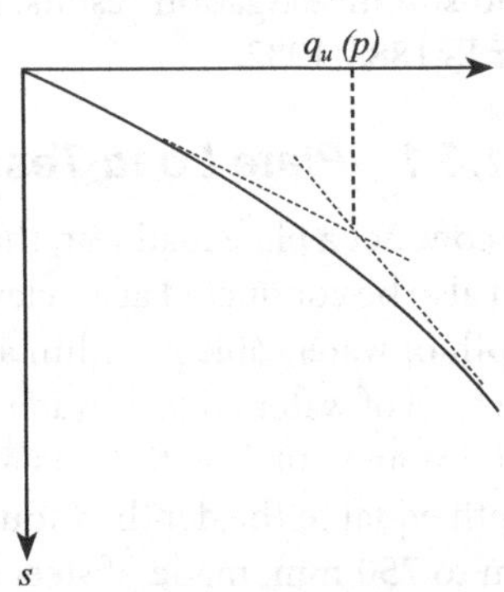

Fig. 4.4: Load intensity vs settlement for plate load test

The following relations can be used for the calculation of ultimate bearing capacity of the proposed foundation $q(f)$:

For clayey soils,

$$q(f) = q_u(p) \quad (4.15)$$

For sandy soils,

$$q_u(f) = q_u(p) \times \frac{B_f}{B_P} \quad (4.16)$$

The plate load test can also be used to calculate the settlement for a given intensity of loading q_O. The following relations can be used between the settlement of the plate (S_p) and that of the foundation (S_f) for the same load intensity:

For clayey soils,

$$S_f = S_P \times \frac{B_f}{B_P} \tag{4.17}$$

where S_p is the settlement of plate, obtained from the load intensity-settlement curve, corresponding to q_O.

For sandy soils,

$$S_f = S_P \left[\frac{B_f (B_P + 0.3)}{B_P (B_f + 0.3)} \right]^2 \tag{4.18}$$

In above equations, B_f is the width of foundation in metres and B_p is the width of the plate also in metres.

Even though the test is widely followed for determining the bearing capacity, plate load test has the following limitations:

- **Size effect:** The results of the plate load test reflect the strength and the settlement characteristics of the soil corresponding to the size of plate. The area where stress is induced in soil is much deeper for the actual foundation when compared to that of the plate and the test does not satisfactorily represent the actual conditions in non- homogeneous and anisotropic soils.
- **Scale effect:** The ultimate bearing capacity of clayey soils is does not depend on the size of the plate but for sandy soils, it increases with the size of the plate (Eq. 4.16). Hence it is advised to repeat the test with plates of different sizes in case of sandy soils.
- **Time effect:** A plate load test is conducted for a short duration when compared with the actual service period of a foundation. In case of clayey soils where consolidation settlement is important, the settlement obtained from the test is not satisfactory.
- **Interpretation of failure load:** The failure load is not well-defined, except in the case of a general shear failure. Hence the load interpreted from the graph highly depends upon the skill of the interpreter.
- **Reaction load:** It is not practicable to provide a reaction of more than 250 kN. Hence, the test on a plate of size larger than 0.6 m width is difficult.
- **Water table:** The level of the water table affects the bearing capacity of the sandy soils. If the depth of water table is within a depth equal to the width of the plate (B_P), the test shall be conducted at the level of water table. If water table is above the test level, it should be lowered to the test level by means of pumping out.

4.1.5.2 Bearing Capacity from Standard Penetration Test

The bearing capacity of foundation can also be calculated using the results of standard penetration test (SPT). The test is conducted before starting the project, at the stage of site investigations, by drilling boreholes. The procedure can be followed as per IS 2131– 1981. Tests shall be made at every change in stratum or at intervals of not more than 1.5 m whichever is less. The intervals be increased to 3 m if in between vane shear test is performed. The test set up consists of a drilling equipment, split spoon sampler and a drive weight assembly. The drive weight assembly shall consist of a driving head and a 63.5 kg weight with 75 cm free fall. The split spoon sampler resting on the bottom of borehole should be allowed to sink under its own weight; then the split spoon sampler shall be first seated 15 cm with the blows of the hammer falling through 75 cm. This first 15 cm is the seating drive. Thereafter, the split spoon sampler shall be further driven by 30 cm more. The number of blows required to affect each 15 cm of penetration shall be recorded. The total blows required for the second and third 15 cm of penetration shall be termed the penetration-resistance N.

The penetration resistance or the SPT N value indicates the resistance of soil to the penetrations induced by the hammer fall, and hence the value can be used for determining the bearing capacity of soils.

Method 1: The ultimate bearing, capacity of sandy soils may be determined using correlations between N and the value of angle of internal friction, φ as mentioned in Table 4.3. The average value of N between the base of the footing and the depth equal to 1.5 to 2.0 times the width of the foundation can be used, and the bearing capacity factors can be found.

Table 4.3: Correlation between N and φ

N	Denseness	φ
0 - 4	Very loose	25° – 32°
4 - 10	Loose	27° – 35°
10 - 30	Medium	30° – 40°
30 - 50	Dense	35° – 45°
> 50	Very dense	> 45°

Method 2: In this method, instead of using correlations between N and φ, the value of N is directly used for determining the bearing capacity. Teng (1962) gave the following equation for the net ultimate capacity of a strip footing:

$$q_{nu} = \frac{1}{6.0}\left[3N^2 B_f W_\gamma + 5\left(100 + N^2\right) D_f W_q\right] \tag{4.19}$$

Or $$q_{nu} = \left[0.5N^2 B_f W_\gamma + 0.83\left(100 + N^2\right) D_f W_q\right] \tag{4.20}$$

4.2 EARTH PRESSURE THEORIES

While foundations transfer the vertical load to the underlying soil, earth retaining structures are required to resist the horizontal stress exerted by soil. Such structures are required when soil has to be retained at different elevations on both sides of a wall. In some cases, soil has to be supported at unsafe slopes, close to vertical, due to space constraints. Retaining structures can be used in such cases as well. Generally, the soil behind retaining structures is vertical, hindering the soil on higher elevation from sliding down. The soil retained is also known as the backfill.

The force acting on retaining structures are in the lateral direction, and the magnitude of this force increases along the depth. The force also depends upon the interaction between the wall and soil, including the friction between them. For simplicity, the retaining wall is assumed to be smooth, vertical and rigid in analysis. The lateral earth pressure is usually computed using the classical theories proposed by Coulomb (1773) and Rankine (1857).

4.2.1 Different Types of Lateral Earth Pressure

Depending upon the movement of the retaining wall with respect to the soil retained, lateral earth pressure is classified into three categories (Fig. 4. 5).

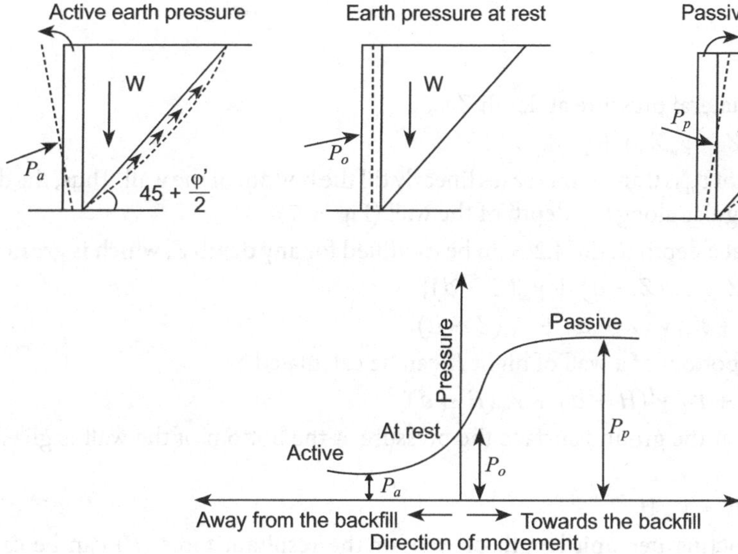

Fig. 4.5: Relationship between lateral earth pressure and wall movement

4.2.1.1 At-rest Pressure

The lateral earth pressure is called at-rest pressure when the retained soil is not subjected to any movement or lateral yielding. This occurs when the retaining wall is firmly fixed at its top without any provisions for rotation and lateral movement. Basement retaining walls and bridge abutments are examples for at rest pressure. This condition is also called the state of elastic equilibrium.

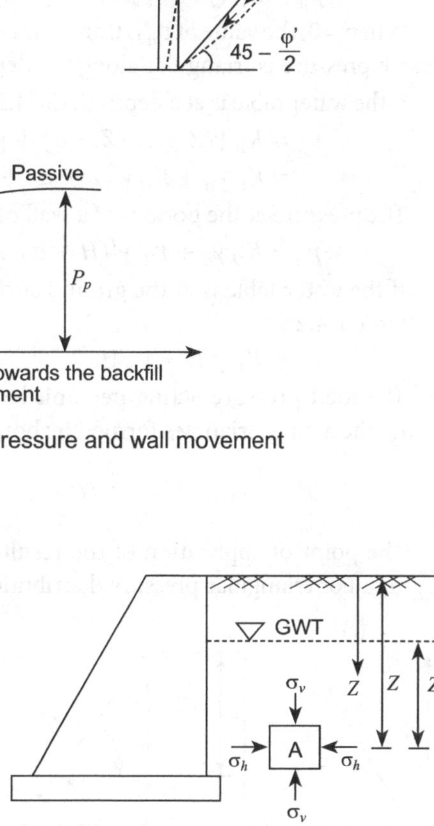

Fig. 4.6: Earth pressure at rest

Fig. 4.6 shows a retaining wall in which no movement takes place. The vertical effective stress at point A at a depth Z is given by

$$\overline{\sigma_v} = \gamma Z - \gamma_w Z_w \tag{4.21}$$

The coefficient of earth pressure at-rest (K_O), is equal to the ratio of the horizontal stress to the vertical stress given by:

$$K_o = \frac{\overline{\sigma_h}}{\overline{\sigma_v}} \tag{4.22}$$

The horizontal effective stress ($\overline{\sigma_h}$) can be obtained by multiplying K_o with $\overline{\sigma_v}$ as:

$$\overline{\sigma_h} = K_O \overline{\sigma_v} = K_O \left(\gamma Z - \gamma_w Z_w\right) \tag{4.23}$$

The coefficient of lateral pressure at rest (K_O) relates the effective stresses. This is because the stress induced by soil in different directions vary, while the hydrostatic stress exerted by pore pressure is same in all directions. Hence pore water pressure should not be multiplied with the coefficient. The total lateral pressure (p_h) is equal to the sum of the effective stress ($P_o = \overline{\sigma_h}$) and the pore water pressure (u).

Thus,

$$p_h = p_o + u \tag{4.24}$$

Therefore, the total lateral pressure at depth Z is,

$$p_h = K_O\,(\gamma Z - \gamma_w Z_w) + \gamma_w Z_w \tag{4.25}$$

When = 0, the value of p_h is 0 and it increases linearly till the bottom of the wall. Thus, the distribution of earth pressure is triangular along the depth of the wall (Fig. 4. 7).

If the water table is at a depth d, Eq. 4.25 can be modified for any depth Z, which is greater than d as:

$$p_h = K_O\,[\gamma Z - \gamma_w(Z - d) + \gamma_w(Z - d)] \tag{4.26}$$

$$= K_O\,\gamma_d + K_O\,\gamma'(Z - d) + \gamma_w(Z - d)$$

The pressure at the bottom of a wall of hight H can be calculated as

$$p_h = K_O\,\gamma_d + K_O\,\gamma'(H - d) + \gamma_w(H - d)$$

If the water table is at the ground surface the pressure at the bottom of the wall is given by, taking $d = 0$ in Eq. 4.26,

$$p_h = K_O\,\gamma' H + \gamma_w \mathrm{H} \tag{4.27}$$

The total pressure acting per unit length of wall, or the resultant force (P) can be calculated by finding the area of triangles formed by both effective stress and pore water pressure.

$$P = \frac{1}{2}(K_O \gamma H^2 + \gamma_w H^2) \tag{4.28}$$

The point of application of the resultant pressure P is determined from the pressure distribution diagram. For triangular pressure distribution, it acts at height $H/3$ from the base.

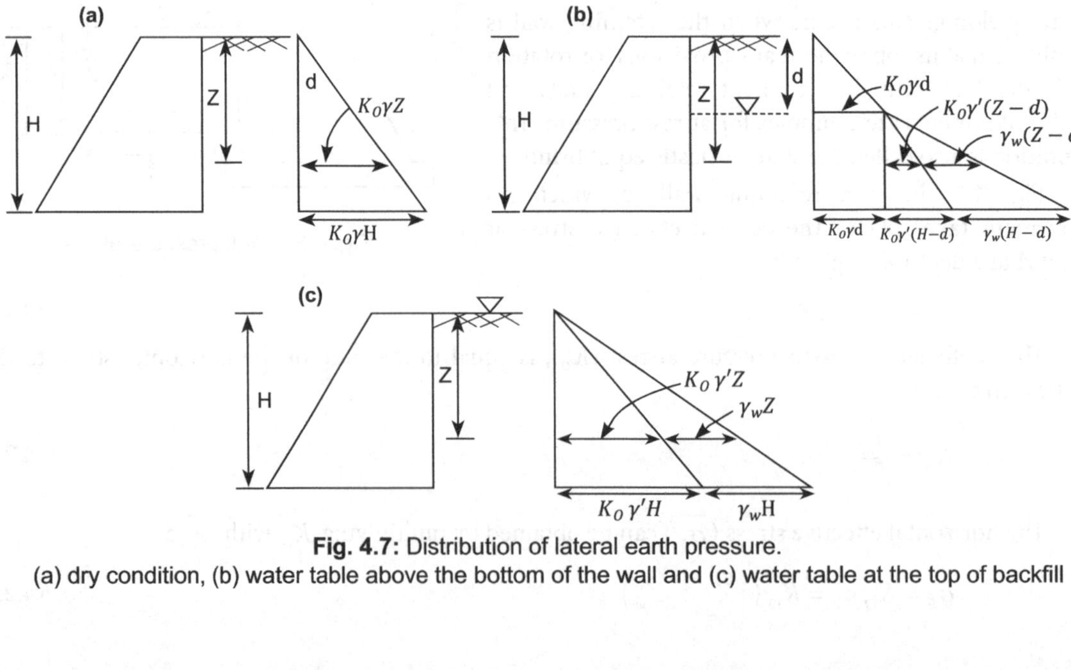

Fig. 4.7: Distribution of lateral earth pressure.
(a) dry condition, (b) water table above the bottom of the wall and (c) water table at the top of backfill

4.2.1.2 Active Pressure

A state of active pressure occurs when the wall moves away from the backfill. It is a state of plastic equilibrium where the backfill soil is on the verge of failure. The soil retained on higher elevation usually exerts pressure on the retaining wall and reaches the state of active earth pressure.

4.2.1.3 Passive Pressure

A state of active pressure occurs when the wall moves towards the back fill. It is another extreme of the limiting equilibrium condition. The state of passive earth pressure exists in soil retained at lower elevation on one side of the backfill. Another example of the passive earth pressure is the pressure acting on an anchor block.

4.2.2 Rankine's Earth Pressure Theory

Rankine (1857) considered the equilibrium of a soil element within a soil mass bounded by a plane surface, based on the following assumptions:

- The soil mass is homogeneous and semi-infinite.
- The soil is dry and cohesionless.
- The ground surface is plane, which may be horizontal or inclined.
- The back of the retaining wall is smooth and vertical.
- The soil element is in a state of plastic equilibrium, ie., at the verge of failure.

The coefficients of active and passive earth pressures can be derived using the concept of Mohrs circle as explained in the following sections.

4.2.2.1 Active Earth Pressure

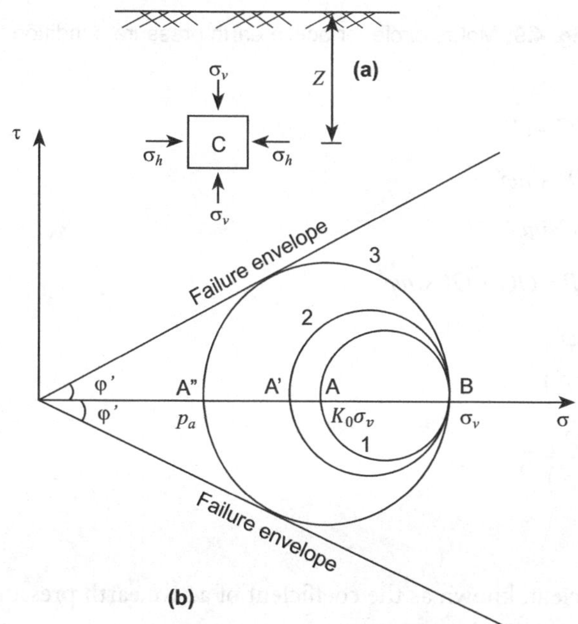

Fig. 4.8: Active earth pressure

Consider an element of dry soil C, at a depth Z below a level soil surface (Fig. 4.8a). Initially, the element is at-rest conditions (circle 1 in Fig. 4. 8b), and the horizontal pressure is given by

$$\sigma_h = K_0\sigma_v$$

where σ_v ($\sigma_v = \gamma Z$)is the vertical stress at C, and K_0 is the coefficient of earth pressure at rest.

The stresses σ_v and σ_h are, respectively, the minor and major principal stresses, and are indicated by points A and B in the Mohr circle (Fig. 4.8b).

When soil stretches horizontally, the vertical stress remains constant, but the horizontal stress is reduced. The point A shifts to position A' and the diameter of the Mohr circle increases. With further decrease in horizontal stress, the point A shifts to position A" when the Mohr circle touches the failure envelope, and the soil is at the verge of failure. This state is known as the Rankine active state of plastic equilibrium, and the horizontal stress at that state is the active pressure (P_a). the Mohr circle when active conditions are developed is plotted in Fig. 4. 9.

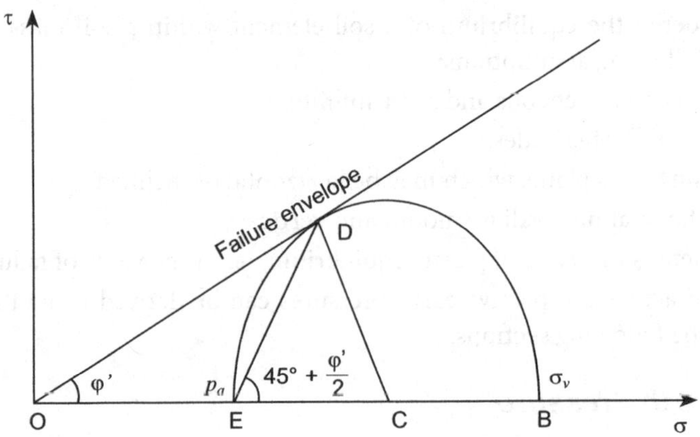

Fig. 4.9: Mohrs circle for active earth pressure condition

From the figure,

$$p_a = OE = OC - CE$$

$$CE = CD = OC sin\varphi',$$

$$p_a = OC - OC sin\varphi'$$

$$\sigma_v = OC + CB = OC + OC sin\varphi'$$

$$\frac{p_a}{\sigma_v} = \frac{(1 - sin\varphi')}{(1 + sin\varphi')}$$

$$p_a = \frac{(1 - sin\varphi')}{(1 + sin\varphi')}\sigma_v$$

$$p_a = K_a \gamma Z$$

where K_a, is a coefficient, known as the coefficient of active earth pressure. It is a function of the angle of shearing resistance (φ'), and is given by

$$K_a = \frac{(1-sin\varphi')}{(1+sin\varphi')} = tan^2\left[45^0 - \frac{\varphi'}{2}\right] \tag{4.29}$$

The pressure distribution is similar to one shown in Fig. 4.7 in which K_a, is substituted for K_o.

4.2.2.2 Passive Earth Pressure

The passive Rankine state of plastic equilibrium can be explained by considering the element of soil at a point at a depth of Z below the soil surface (Fig. 4.10a).

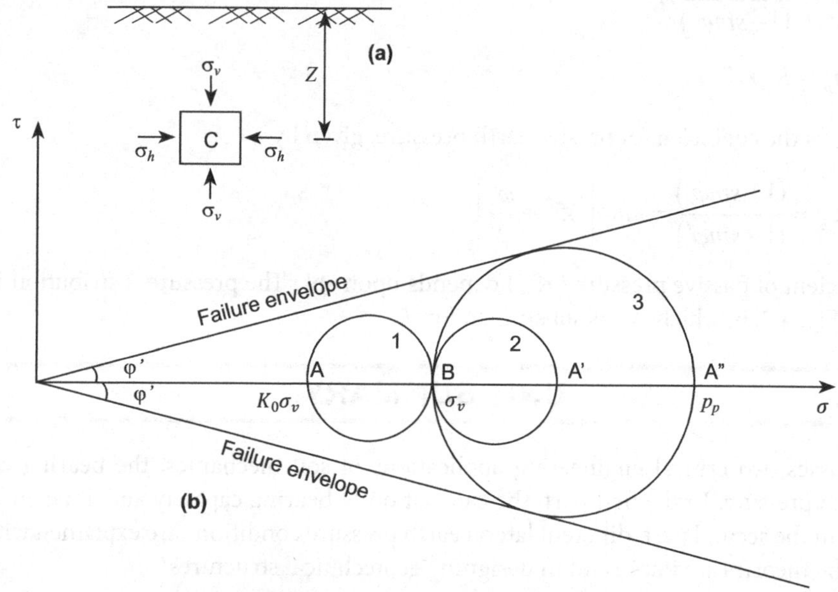

Fig. 4.10: Passive earth pressure

As the soil is compressed laterally, the horizontal stress is increased, whereas the vertical stress remains constant. The Mohr circles in Fig. 4.10b plots the variation from at rest to failure. At the verge of failure, the horizontal stress increases until it reaches a limiting value greater than the vertical stress, indicated by point A" and the Mohr circle touches the failure envelope. Fig. 4.11, shows the Mohr circle at failure.

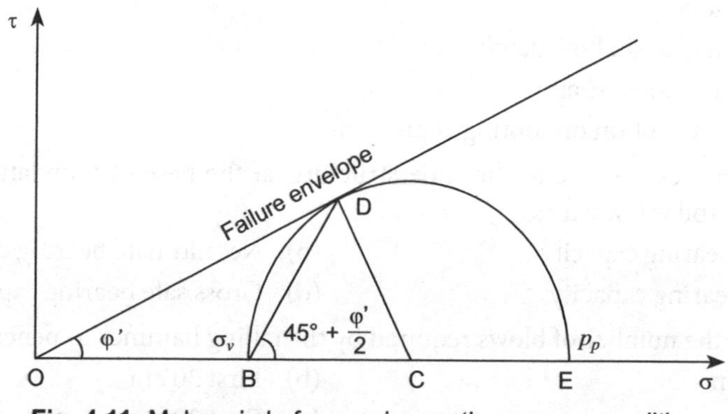

Fig. 4.11: Mohrs circle for passive earth pressure condition

From Fig. 4.11,

$$p_p = OC + CE = OC + CD = OC + OC\,sin\varphi'$$

$$\sigma_v = OC - BC = OC - CD = OC - OC\,sin\varphi'$$

$$\frac{p_p}{\sigma_v} = \frac{(1+sin\varphi')}{(1-sin\varphi')}$$

$$p_p = \frac{(1+sin\varphi')}{(1-sin\varphi')}\sigma_v$$

$$p_p = K_p \gamma Z$$

where K_p is the coefficient of passive earth pressure, given by

$$K_p = \frac{(1+sin\varphi')}{(1-sin\varphi')} = tan^2\left[45^0 + \frac{\varphi'}{2}\right] \tag{4.30}$$

The coefficient of passive pressure (K_p) depends upon Φ'. The pressure distribution is similar to that shown in Fig. 4.7, in which K_p is substituted for K_O

UNIT SUMMARY

The unit discusses two critical engineering applications of soil mechanics, the bearing capacity and the lateral earth pressure. In the first part, the calculation of bearing capacity and Terzaghi's theory are discussed and in the second part, different lateral earth pressure conditions are explained with Rankine's theory. Both the theories are important in designing geotechnical structures/

EXERCISES

Multiple Choice Questions

1. Which among the following is not an assumption in Terzaghi's bearing capacity theory?
   (a) Footing is long
   (b) Footing is laid at shallow depth
   (c) Footing is in square shape
   (d) The load distribution on footing is uniform
2. The increase in pressure due to the superstructure, at the base of foundation that leads to the shear failure of soil is known as:
   (a) Ultimate bearing capacity (b) Net ultimate bearing capacity
   (c) Net safe bearing capacity (d) Gross safe bearing capacity
3. SPT *N* value is the number of blows required by the falling hammer to penetrate
   (a) First 15 cm (b) First 30 cm
   (c) Last 30 cm (d) First 30 cm

4. Which among the following arrangements is correct in terms of magnitude of lateral earth pressure, when the vertical stress and other conditions remains constant?
   (a) Active earth pressure > Passive earth pressure > Earth pressure at rest
   (b) Active earth pressure > Earth pressure at rest > Passive earth pressure
   (c) Passive earth pressure > Active earth pressure > Earth pressure at rest
   (d) Passive earth pressure > Earth pressure at rest > Active earth pressure

Answers of Multiple Choice Questions			
1. (c)	2. (b)	3. (c)	4. (d)

Numerical Examples

1. The strip footing below a wall is placed at ground level, with a width of 2 m. The soil is dry sand with a unit weight of 19 kN/m³ and angle of internal friction 40°. Calculate the ultimate bearing capacity of the footing.

$$B = 2m$$

$$D_f = 0m$$

$$\gamma = 19 \text{ kN/m}^3$$

$$\varphi' = 40^o$$

$$c' = 0kPa$$

$$N_q = 81.3$$

$$N_\gamma = 100.4$$

$$q_u = c'N_c + \gamma D_f N_q + 0.5B\gamma N_\gamma$$

$$= 0 + 0 + 0.5 \times 2 \times 19 \times 100.4$$

$$= 197.6 kN/m^2$$

2. Determine the ultimate bearing capacity of a strip footing 1.5 m wide, placed at a depth of 1m. The soil has a cohesion of 15 kPa, angle of internal friction 35°, unit weight 18 kN/m³. Consider depth of water table at:
   a. Ground surface
   b. 1 m below the ground surface
   c. 10 m below the ground surface

$$B = 1.5m$$

$$D_f = 1m$$

$$\gamma = 18 \text{ kN/m}^3$$

$$\varphi' = 35^o$$

$$c' = 15kPa$$

$$N_c = 57.8$$

$N_q = 41.8$

$N_\gamma = 42.4$

$q_u = c'N_c + \gamma D_f N_q W_q + 0.5B\gamma N_\gamma W_\gamma$

a. Water Table at ground surface

$W_q = W_\gamma = 0.5$

$q_u = c'N_c + \gamma D_f N_q W_q + 0.5B\gamma N_\gamma W_\gamma$

$= 15 \times 57.8 + 18 \times 1 \times 41.8 \times 0.5 + 0.5 \times 1.5 \times 18 \times 42.4 \times 0.5$

$= 1529.4 kN/m^2$

b. Water Table 1 m below ground surface

$W_\gamma = 0.5$

$$W_q = 1 - 0.5\left(\frac{D_f - D_w}{D_f}\right) = 1$$

$q_u = c'N_c + \gamma D_f N_q W_q + 0.5B\gamma N_\gamma W_\gamma$

$= 15 \times 57.8 + 18 \times 1 \times 41.8 \times 1 + 0.5 \times 1.5 \times 18 \times 42.4 \times 0.5$

$= 1905.6 kN/m^2$

c. Water Table 10 m below ground surface

$W_q = W_\gamma = 1$

$q_u = c'N_c + \gamma D_f N_q W_q + 0.5B\gamma N_\gamma W_\gamma$

$= 15 \times 57.8 + 18 \times 1 \times 41.8 \times 1 + 0.5 \times 1.5 \times 18 \times 42.4 \times 1$

$= 2191.8 kN/m^2$

3. A 6.3 m high vertical wall with smooth surface retains loose sand with bulk unit weight of 18 kN/m³ and angle of internal friction 18°. The backfill has the same height of wall and the surface of backfill is horizontal. Determine the total active thrust on the wall and its point of application, if the water table is well below the base of the wall.

$\gamma = 18 \text{ kN/m}^3$

$\varphi' = 18^o$

$H = 6.3m$

$$K_a = \frac{(1 - sin\varphi')}{(1 + sin\varphi')} = tan^2\left[45^0 - \frac{\varphi'}{2}\right]$$

$= 0.53$

At the surface of backfill,

$p_a = 0$

At the bottom of the wall,

$$p_a = K_a \gamma Z = K_a \gamma H$$
$$= 0.53 \times 18 \times 6.3$$
$$= 59.86 kN/m^2$$
$$P_a = \frac{1}{2}(K_a \gamma H^2)$$
$$= \frac{1}{2}\left(0.53 \times 18 \times 6.3^2\right)$$
$$= 189.32 kN/m$$

Point of action of P_a from the bottom of the wall,

$$y = H/3$$
$$= 2.1m$$

Exercises

1. Two footings, one circular and the other square, are resting on the surface of a purely cohesionless soil. If both the foundations are having same base area, the ratio of their (circular to square) ultimate bearing capacities as per Terzaghi's theory is:
2. Determine the net safe bearing capacity for a square footing (2m x 2m) resting at a depth of 2m, when the water table is
   a. at ground surface.
   b. 1m below the ground surface.
   c. At the base of the footing
   d. 5m below the ground surface.

   Use Terzaghi's equation.

   The density of the soil is 18 kN/m³, saturated density is 20 kN/m³, c = 5 kN/m², $\varphi = 40^o$
3. For the retaining walls shown in figure, determine the active earth thrust per unit length of the wall. Also determine the location of the resultant force.

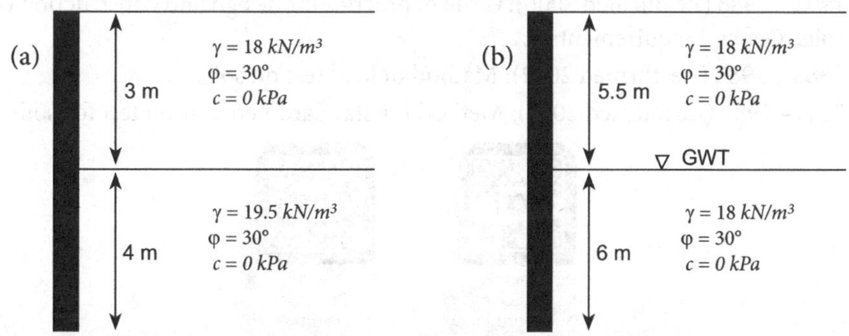

Short and Long Answer Type Questions

1. What are the assumptions made in Terzaghi's bearing capacity theory?
2. Define the following terms:

(a) Ultimate bearing capacity
(b) Net safe bearing capacity
(c) Net allowable bearing pressure

3. What is meant by consolidation settlement? Is it observed in sandy soils? Justify our answer.
4. What is a standard penetration test?
5. What are the different categories of lateral earth pressure? Explain with a neat sketch.
6. Derive the equation for coefficient of active earth pressure using Rankine's theory, for cohesionless soils.
7. How is ultimate bearing capacity calculated using plate load test? Explain in detail.
8. What are the different types of shear failures that may occur in a foundation? Explain with neat sketches.
9. Write down the assumptions and limitations of Rankine's Earth Pressure theory.

KNOW MORE

Foundation and retaining wall failures are increasing in India. Earth work should be considered as an engineering work and when quality control is not assured, the designed properties are not achieved in the field, and as a result, designed strength is not achieved. Extreme climatic events are also another major reason for the recent geotechnical failures, where seepage has resulted in foundation failures, further leading to the failure of the structure. It is suggested to do a detailed case study on the retaining wall failures happened in India after 2020 and find out the reasons for failure.

REFERENCES AND SUGGESTED READINGS

- Arora,K.R., "Soil Mechanics and Foundation Engineering," Standard Publishers Distributors, Delhi, 2008.
- Gulhati, S. K.; Datta, M." Geotechnical engineering, Tata McGraw-Hill, New Delhi, 2005.
- IS 1904 – 1986 (Reaffirmed 2006): Code of practice for design and construction of foundations in soils: General requirements.
- IS 1888 – 1982 (Reaffirmed 2002): Method of load test on soils
- IS 2131– 1981 (Reaffirmed 2002): Method for standard penetration test for soils

Dynamic QR Code for Further Reading

Dynamic QR Code for Further Reading

5 Compaction and Stabilization of Soil

UNIT SPECIFICS

Through this unit we shall discuss the following aspects:

- Concept of compaction
- Compaction tests
- Factors affecting compaction
- Field compaction
- Soil stabilization
- Site investigations

RATIONALE

This unit on the compaction and stabilization of soil deals with the process of compaction in soil, and the factors affecting compaction. Compaction is a useful process in densifying the soil, by removing air voids. By knowing the compaction curves of a soil sample, it is possible to understand the optimum moisture content, and to achieve the maximum dry density. Compaction is usually carried out before the commencement of construction, using rollers and vibrators. There are different ground improvement techniques which uses the concept of compaction, for improving the soil strength at surface and deep levels. This chapter also discusses the need for such soil stabilisation techniques, and the methods of site investigation that should be carried out before starting any construction activities.

PRE-REQUISITES

- Soil classification,
- Index properties.

UNIT OUTCOMES

List of outcomes of this unit is as follows:

U5-O1: Learn the concept of compaction and the tests for determining optimum moisture content and maximum dry density

U5-O2: Understand the factors affecting compaction and the field methos of compaction.

U5-O3: Learn the process of soil stabilization and its necessity.

U5-O4: Understand the significance of California Bearing Ratio in pavement construction.

U5-O5: Learn the types of soil exploration and field identification of soil.

Unit-5 Outcomes	EXPECTED MAPPING WITH COURSE OUTCOMES (1- Weak Correlation; 2- Medium correlation; 3- Strong Correlation)				
	CO-1	CO-2	CO-3	CO-4	CO-5
U5-O1	-	-	-	-	3
U5-O2	-	-	-	-	3
U5-O3	-	-	-	-	3
U5-O4	-	-	-	-	3
U5-O5	2	-	-	-	3

5.1 COMPACTION

Compaction is the process in which soil partials are artificially rearranged and packed together into closer state of contact by mechanical means in order to reduce void ratio, permeability and compressibility and in order to increase the degree of denseness, stability, shear strength and bearing capacity.

In 1933, Proctor showed that there existed a definite relationship between the soil water content and degree of dry density to which a soil might be compacted. The compaction characteristics are first determined in a laboratory by various compaction tests. These tests are based on any one of the following methods or type of compaction: dynamic or impact, kneading, static and vibration. Some of the usual compaction test used in laboratory to determine water density relationship of soils are: Standard and modified proctor tests, Harvard miniature compaction test, Abbot Compaction test and Jodhpur-mini compactor test. During a compaction test, the density of soil is measured at different water contents, after doing compaction. Standard proctor test and modified proctor tests are followed in India with minor modifications, as light compaction and heavy compaction respectively, as per IS 2720, for different field applications.

5.1.1 Light Compaction

The procedure for light compaction, with minor modifications from the standard proctor test is described in IS 2720 (Part VII). The test equipment consists of a cylindrical metal mould, detachable base plate and collar in effective height and a rammer of 2.6 kg in mass falling through a height of 310 mm. The test consists of compacting soil at various water contents in the mould, in three equal layers, each layer being given 25 blows of the rammer. Before putting the second layer of soil, the top of the first compacted layer is scratched with the help of any sharp edge. The second and third layers are similarly compacted, each layer being given 25 blows. The last compacted layer should project not more than 6 mm into the collar. The collar is removed, and the excess soil is trimmed off to make it level with the top of mould. A soil sample from the centre of the compacted specimen is then kept for water content determination. Fig. 5. 1 shows the dimensions of the test mould and the rammer as per IS code.

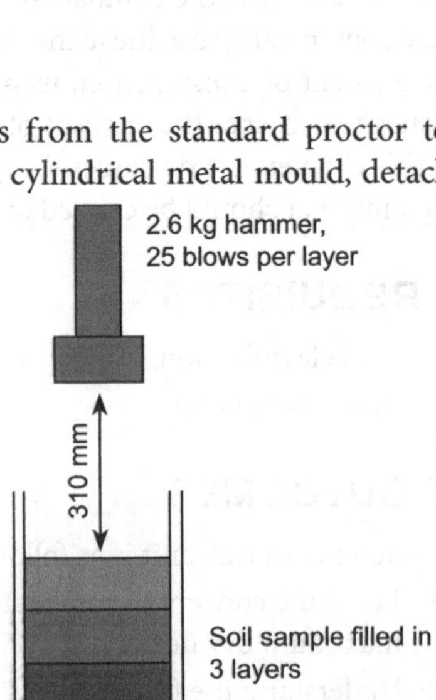

Fig. 5.1: Set up for light compaction as per IS 2720 (Part VII)

The dry density obtained in each test is determined by knowing the mass of the compacted soil and its water content. The bulk density ρ and the corresponding dry density ρ_d for the compacted soil are calculated from the following relations:

$$\rho = \frac{M}{V}; \rho_d = \frac{\rho}{1+w}\left(g/cm^3\right) \tag{5.1}$$

where M is the mass of compacted soil, V is the volume of mould and w is the water content.

5.1.2 Heavy Compaction

Higher compaction is needed for heavier transport and military aircraft. The modified proctor test was developed to give a higher standard of compaction. This test was standardized by the American Association of State Highway Officials and is known as the modified AASHO test. In heavy compaction, the soil is compacted in the same mould used for light compaction, but in five layers, each layer being given 25 blows of a 4.9 kg rammer dropped through a height of 450 mm as per IS: 2720 (Part VIII) – 1983. Similar to the case of light compaction, the sample is weight after removing the excess portion after removing the collar, and a sample from the centre of the specimen is kept for water content determination.

The dry density is calculated using Eq. 5.1. The process of plotting the compaction curve is mentioned in the next section.

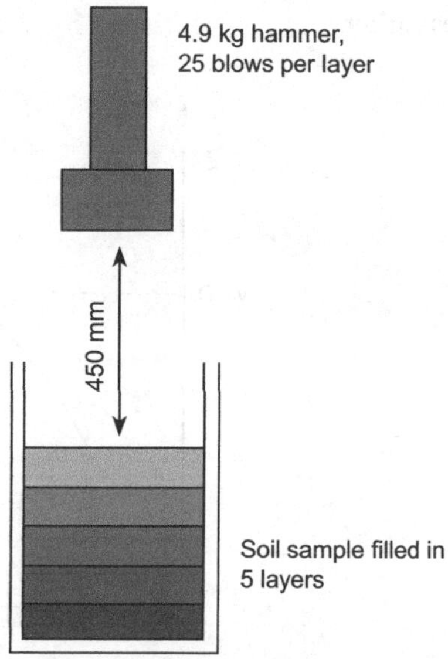

Fig. 5.2: Set up for heavy compaction as per IS 2720 (Part VIII)

The differences in volume of samples, weight of hammer and number of layers used in different compaction tests are listed below in Table 5. 1.

Table 5.1: Comparison between different compaction tests

	Standard proctor test	IS 2720 Light Compaction test	Modified Proctor test	IS 2720 Heavy Compaction Test
Volume of Mould (cm^3)	945	1000	945	1000
Number of Layers	3	3	5	5
number of blows	25	25	25	25
Weight of Hammer (kg)	2.495	2.6	4.54	4.9
Height of freefall (mm)	304.5	310	457.4	450

5.1.3 Plotting Compaction Curve

During a compaction test, the whole procedure of compaction, till the determination of dry density is repeated multiple times, with varying water content. The first trial starts with lowest water content, and it should be increased gradually. Initially, the weight of compacted soil goes on increasing with increase in moisture content, but after a certain limit, it starts decreasing. The test should be continued till this drop is noted. The dry density of soil is calculated for each trial. The plot between water content (abscissa) and dry density (ordinate) is then plotted, which is known as the compaction curve, as shown in Fig. 5.3. The dry density increases as the water content is increased, till maximum dry density (MDD) is reached. The water content corresponding to the maximum density is called the optimum moisture content (OMC).

When the water content is lower than OMC,the soil is stiff and has more void spaces. This results in lower dry density. With the increase in water content, soil particles get rearranged into densely packed positions, and this results in an increase in dry density. When water content is increased beyond OMC, the dry density is reduced as the excess water occupies the space that might have been occupied by solid particles earlier.

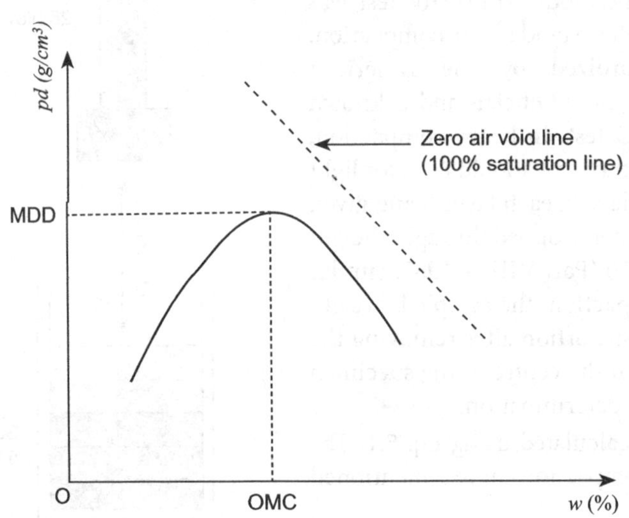

Fig. 5.3: Compaction curve

5.1.3.1 Zero Air Void Line

A line which shows the water content dry density relationship for the compacted soil containing a constant percentage air voids is known as an air voids lines and can be established from the following relations:

$$\rho_d = \frac{(1-n_a)G\rho_w}{1+wG} \tag{5.2}$$

where n_a is the percentage air voids, G is the specific gravity of soil and ρ_w is the density of water.

The theoretical maximum compaction for any given water content corresponds to the zero air voids conditions. The line showing the dry density as a function of water content for soil containing no air voids is called the zero air voids line or the saturated soil when $n_a = 0$ in Eq. 5.2, as:

$$\rho_{d(theoretical)} = \frac{G\rho_w}{1+wG} \tag{5.3}$$

In heavy compaction, the water content dry density curve lies above that of light compaction, and has its peak relatively placed towards the left. Thus, for a same soil, heavier compaction results in increased MDD value at a lower water content (Fig. 5.4).

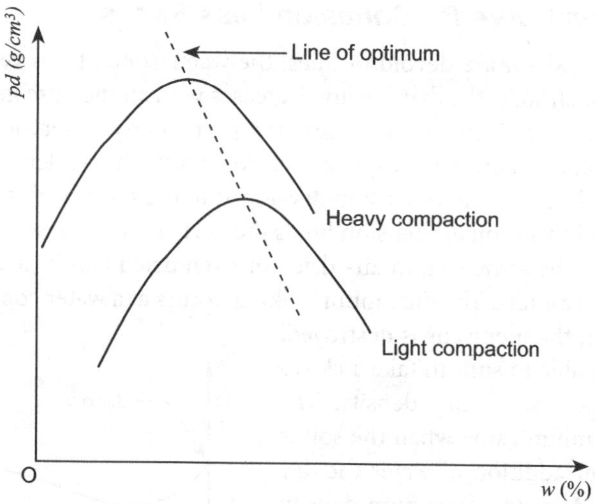

Fig. 5.4: Compaction curves for light compaction and heavy compaction

The soil with water content less than OMC is said to be in the dry side of optimum, and the soil with water content more that OMC is said to be in the wet side of optimum. The important properties of soil (relative) in both these conditions are listed below in Table 5.2.

Table 5.2: Some important properties and its side of optimum

Properties	Dry of optimum	Wet of optimum
Structure of soil	Flocculent	Dispersed
Permeability	More	Less
Pore water pressure	Less	More
Swelling	More	Less
Shrinkage	Less	More
Strength	More	Less
Compressibility		
Low stress compressibility	Less	More
High stress compressibility	More	Less

The degree of compaction and moisture content of the soil for different field applications are decided based on the properties listed in Table 5. 2. The soil in the core of earthen dam and pavement subgrade is usually compacted in the wet side of optimum. While less permeable soil is required in the case of earthen dam, less compressibility and swelling properties are required in the case of pavement subgrade. A homogenous earthen dam is compacted in the dry side of optimum, as it requires soil with more strength.

Compaction test is more significant in the case of cohesive soils. In the case of sandy soil, the variation of dry density with water content is not as significant as that in the case of clay.

5.1.3.2 Compaction Curve for Cohesion Less Sands

In the case of sandy soils which are devoid of fines, the water content has very little influence on the compacted density. For such soils, the dry density decreases with an increase in the water content, in the initial in the water content, in the initial stage of the curve, particularly under a low compaction effect. This is due to the bulking of sands wherein the capillary tension resists the tendency of soil particles to take a dense state. In other words, the capillary tension developed in the sandy soil is not fully counteracted by the comp active effort and this capillary tension holds the particles in a loose state resisting compaction. Is interesting to note that the same soil, in air- dried or oven dried condition, achieves greater density under the same compactive effort. The maximum bulking occurs at a water content between 4 to 5%. On further addition of water, the meniscus is destroyed, and the soil particles are able to shift to take a closer packing, resulting in increase in dry density. The density reaches the maximum value when the soil is fully saturated on further addition of water the dry density again decreases. Also, the maximum density attained under full saturation condition, is not very much higher than that corresponding to air dried or oven dried condition. Secondly, the attainment of maximum density at full saturation is not due to lubrication action of water but rather it is due to the reduction of effective pressure between soil particles by hydrostatic pressure. Such soils do not display distinct optimum water content (Fig. 5.5).

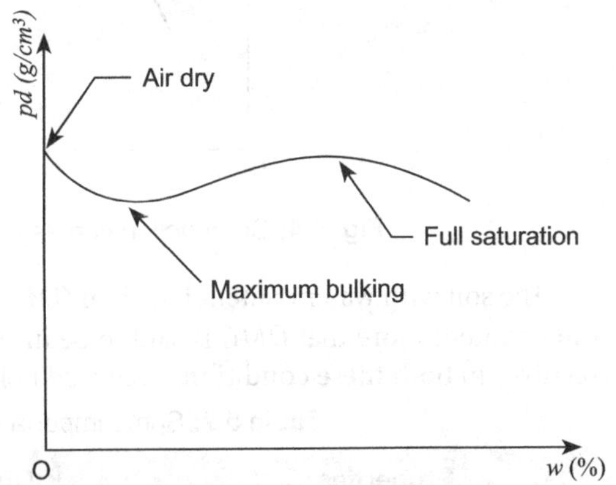

Fig. 5.5: Compaction curve for cohesionless soils

5.1.4 Factors Affecting Compaction

The various factors which affect the compacted density are as follows:

5.1.4.1 Water Content

It has been seen by laboratory experiments that as the water is increased, the compacted density goes on increasing; till a maximum dry density is achieved after which further addition of water decreases the density. When only a relatively small amount of water is present in soil, it is firmly held by the electrical forces at the surface of soil particles with a high concentration of electrolyte which prevents the diffuse double layer surrounding the particles from developing fully. The double layer depression leads to a low inter- particle repulsion and the particles do not move over on mother easily when compactive energy is applied and high percentage air voids and low density is achieved. The increase in water content results in an expansion of double layer and a reduction in the net attractive forces between particles or in a increased inter-particle repulsion which permits the particles to slide more easily past one other into a more oriented and denser state of packing together, and hence higher density. After the optimum water content is reached, the air voids approach approximately a constant value as further increase in water content does not cause any appreciable decrease in them, even though a more orderly arrangement of particles may exist at higher water contents. The total voids due to water and air combination go on increasing with increase of water content beyond the optimum and hence the dry density of the soils falls.

5.1.4.2 Amount of Compaction

The amount of compaction greatly affects the maximum dry density and optimum water content of a given soil. The effect of increasing the compactive energy results in an increase in the maximum dry density and decrease in the optimum water content. However, the increase in maximum dry density does not have linear relationship with increase of compacted effort.

5.1.4.3 Method of compaction

The density obtained during compaction, for a given soil, greatly depends upon the type of compaction or the way compactive effort is applied. The various variables in the aspect are (i) weight of the compacting equipment, (ii) the manner of operation such as dynamic or impact, static kneading or rolling and (iii) time and area of contact between the compacting element and the soil.

5.1.4.4 Type of Soil

The maximum dry density achieved corresponding to a given compactive energy largely depends upon the type of soil. Well graded coarse-grained soils attain a much higher density and lower optimum water contents then fine-grained soils which require more water for lubrication because of the greater specific surface.

5.1.4.5 Addition of Admixtures

The compaction properties/characteristics of soil can be modified by a number of admixtures other than soil material. These admixtures have special application in stabilised soil construction.

5.1.5 Suitability of Various Compaction Equipment

Compaction can be done at both shallow and deep depth. The compaction at shallow depths or surface compaction is widely carried out as a part of ground improvement and for pavements. Surface compaction can be carried out by three methods, rolling, ramming and vibration.

5.1.5.1 Roller

The compaction achieved by rollers depend upon their contact pressure, number of passes, layer thickness and speed of roller. While the compaction increases with contact pressure and number of passes, it decreases with an increase in layer thickness. The speed of roller should be optimized for the application required. Different types of rollers (Fig. 5. 6) are used for compaction as listed below:

- Smooth wheel roller
  - Compaction is achieved by application of pressure over the soil.
  - Suitable for coarse grained soil like gravel, crushed stone and sand etc.
  - Generally used in construction of road.
- Sheep foot roller:
  - Compaction is carried out by kneading action which provide comparatively strong bond between compacted layers of soil.
  - Suitable for cohesive soil.
  - Used in construction of earthen dam.

- Pneumatic tyred roller
    - Compaction is carried out by the combined action of pressure and needing.
    - Suitable for all types of soil but generally preferred for cohesive soil.
    - Used in construction of roadway, airfield and homogeneous dams.

Smooth wheel roller Sheep foot roller Pneumatic tyre roller

Fig. 5.6: Different types of rollers

5.1.5.2 Rammer

Rammers or tampers are used to compact the soil under the effect of impact. Rammers are generally preferred for cohesive soil. They are used for compacting soil in confined areas such as near to retaining walls, basement walls etc.

5.1.5.3 Vibrator

In this approach, vibrations are induced in soil during compaction. This method is best suited for compaction of sand. This method is widely used for compacting soil in confined areas and in construction of embankment of oil storage tanks.

5.1.6 Difference Between Compaction and Consolidation

Both compaction and consolidation are processes in which soil particles get rearranged into a denser arrangement. Even though the ultimate result is reduction in volume, both processes are entirely different. He differences between compaction and consolidation are listed in Table 5. 3 below:

Table 5.3: Difference between compaction and consolidation

Compaction	Consolidation
It is almost instantaneous process.	It is time dependent process.
Soil is in unsaturated condition.	Soil is completely saturated.
Volume reduction due to expulsion of air from void spaces.	Volume reduction is due to expulsion of pore water.
Specified mechanical techniques are used in the process (like roller, rammer and vibrator)	Consolidation occurs on account of a load placed on soil.

5.2 SOIL STABILIZATION

Stabilization in a broad sense, incorporates the various methods employed for modification the properties of a soil to improve its engineering performance. Stabilization is being used for a variety of engineering works, the most common application being in the construction of road and airfield pavements, where the main objective is to increase the strength or stability of soil and to reduced construction cost by making best use of locally available material.

Methods of stabilization may be grouped under two main types:

- Modification or improvement of a soil property of the existing soil without any admixture.
- Modifications of the properties of soil by using admixtures.

5.2.1.1 Mechanical Stabilisation

Two processes are involved in mechanical stabilization: (i) composition by adding or removing specific components, and (ii) densification or compaction. The key elements influencing a soil's engineering behaviour are its composition and particle size distribution. A suitable soil fraction can be added or removed to significantly alter the characteristics. The soil components can be split into two fractions for mechanical stabilization, where the main goal is to have a soil that is resistant to deformation and displacement under loads: the granular fraction kept on a 75 micron IS sieve and the fine soil fraction passing through a 75-micron sieve. Strength and hardness are imparted by the granular fraction. The fine fraction provides cohesion or binding property, water-retention capacity and also acts as a filler for the voids of the coarse fraction. *Mechanical stabilisation has been largely used in the construction* of economical roads.

5.2.1.2 Cement Stabilisation

The soil stabilised with cement (Portland) is known as soil cement. The cementing action is believed to be the result of chemical reaction of cement with the silicious soil during hydration. The binding action of individual particles through cement may be possible only in coarse-grained soils. In fine grained, cohesive soils, only some of the particles can be expected to have cement bonds, and the rest will be bonded through natural cohesion. The important factors affecting soil cement are nature of soil, cement content, conditions of mixing, compaction and curing, and admixtures.

5.2.1.3 Lime Stabilisation

Heavy, deformable clayey soils can be effectively treated with hydrated (or slaked) lime. Lime can be used on its own or in conjunction with fly ash, bitumen, or cement. These combinations can also stabilize sandy soils. The main use of lime has been to stabilize the sub-grades and road bases. Two types of chemical reactions happen when lime is added to soil: (1) base exchange phenomenon changes the composition of the absorbed layer, and (2) cementing or pozzolanic activity. High plasticity soils become less plastic to handle and pulverize when lime is added to the mixture. In case of soils with low plasticity, their plasticity index increases.

5.2.1.4 Bitumen Stabilisation

Bituminous materials like asphalts and tars are typically used to build pavements and stabilize soil. Normally, these substances are too viscous to be mixed in with soil. Asphalts can be made more fluid by heating, emulsifying, or using a cut-back procedure. Tars are either heated or reduced. When added to soil, bituminous materials have a cohesion or binding effect and inhibit water absorption. Therefore, for stabilization, either the binding action, the water proofing action, or both of these actions may be used. Bitumen stabilization is divided into four categories based on these actions and the makeup of the soils: (i) sand-bitumen; (ii) soil-bitumen; (iii) water- proofed mechanical stabilization; and (iv) oiled earth.

5.2.1.5 Chemical Stabilisation

Chemical stabilizers, commonly referred to as soil binders or soil palliatives, help to stabilize soil temporarily. They are easily applied to the soil's surface, can stabilize regions where vegetation cannot grow, and offer strong resistance against wind and runoff erosion.

Chemical stabilizers can be divided into the following categories: concentrated liquid stabilizer, water with surfactant, water-absorbing, synthetic polymer emulsion, organic non-petroleum, organic petroleum, and clay additive.

5.2.1.6 Stabilisation by Heating

Heating a fine-grained soil to temperatures of the order of 400 to 600° C makes it non-plastic, less water sensitive irreversible changes in clay minerals. Also, the clay clods get converted into aggregates. Soil can be baked in kilns, or in-situ downwards draft slow-moving furnaces. The artificial aggregates so produced can be used for mechanical stabilisation.

5.2.1.7 Electrical Stabilisation

The stability or shear strength of fine-grained soils can be increased by draining them with the passage of direct current through them. The process is also known as electro-osmosis. Electrical drainage is accompanied by electro-chemical composition of the electrodes and the deposition of the metal salts in the soil pores. There may also be some changes in the structure of soil. The resulting cementing of soil due to all these reactions, is also known as electro-chemical hardening and for this purpose the use of aluminium anodes is recommended.

5.2.1.8 Reinforced Earth and Geosynthetics

The term "Geosynthetics" has been proposed in 1983 by J.E. Fleut, Jr. collectively all synthetic materials, including geomembranes. They have multiple applications in geotechnical engineering. A geosynthetic can increase the tensile strength of a soil through interface shear strength. It can also act as a tensioned membrane when it is placed between two materials, which, in effect, is the reinforcement function of the geosynthetic, with tensile strength as its key property. They can also be used for accelerated drainage in fine grained soils.

5.3 CALIFORNIA BEARING RATIO (CBR) TEST

The CBR test is penetration test meant for the evaluation of subgrade strength of roads and pavements. The results obtained by these tests are used with the empirical curves to determine the thickness of pavement and its component layers. This is the most widely used method for the design of flexible pavement. The procedure is explained in IS 2720 (Part XVI)- 1987.

CBR is defined as the ratio expressed in percentage of force per unit area needed to penetrate a soil mass with a standard plunger of 50 mm diameter at the rate of 1.25 mm/min to that required for corresponding penetration in a standard material. The standard material is crushed stone and the load which has been obtained from a test on it is the standard load, this material is considered to have a CBR of 100%. The ratio is usually determined for penetration of 2.5 and 5 mm. When the ratio at 5 mm is consistently higher than that at 2.5 mm, the ratio at 5 mm is used.

Table 5. 4 gives the standard loads adopted for different penetrations for the standard material with a C.B.R. value of 100%.

Table 5.4: Penetration vs standard load for CBR

Penetration Depth (mm)	Standard Load (kg)
2.5	1370
5	2055

The test apparatus consists of loading machine with minimum 5000 kg capacity with a movable head or base which enables the standard plunger of 50 mm diameter to penetrate the specimen at a rate of 1.25 mm/min. The mould used is cylindrical, with a detachable metal extension collar and a detachable perforated base plate. A circular metal spacer disc is also provided. A While using a remoulded specimen, the sample should be compacted at either the value of MDD and

OMC estimated by the heavy compaction test or the field density and natural moisture content. Compact the mix soil in the mould using heavy compaction, in five layers, but with 56 blows for each layer. The collar of the mould can be then removed to level the surface. The penetration can then be conducted on soaked or unsoaked samples. For soaking, the specimen within the mould is covered with filter papers and perforated plate and a surcharge weight equivalent to the pavement is added. The mould assembly and loads are then immersed in water for 96 hours.

For the penetration test, the sample is placed in the loading machine and the load is applied at a rate of 1.25 mm/min. The load readings at penetrations of 0.5, 1.0, 1.5, 2.0, 2.5, 4.0, 5.0, 7.5, 10 and 12.5 mm should be recorded. A graph is then plotted between load (ordinate) and penetration (abscissa), and if the curve has a concave shape close to the abscissa, it has to be corrected as per Fig. 5. 7. The CBR value (corresponding to 2.5 mm or 5 mm) is then calculated as:

$$CBR = \frac{\text{Test load}}{\text{Standard load}} \times 100 \tag{5.4}$$

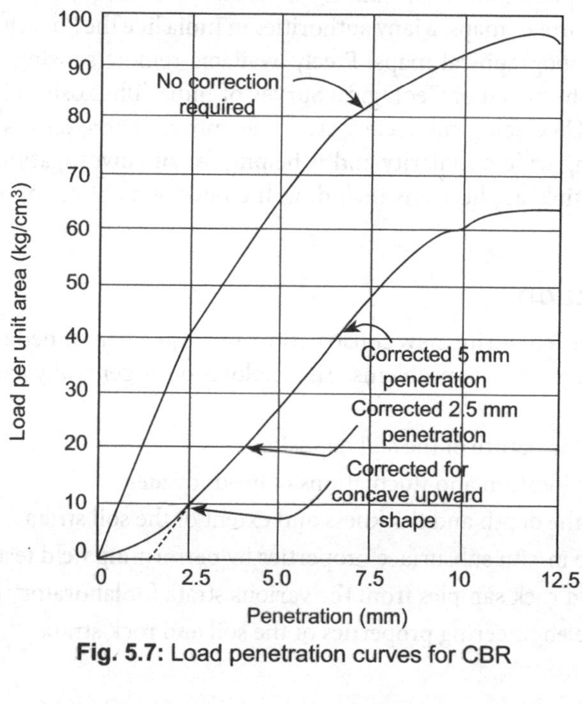

Fig. 5.7: Load penetration curves for CBR

The CBR value can be used as an index of soil strength and its bearing capacity. The test is highly helpful to determine the strength of the subgrade soil and select a suitable pavement thickness for the expected traffic. The results obtained from the CBR test are used with the design curves developed by different authorities to determine the thickness of pavement and various component layers of pavement.

5.4 SITE INVESTIGATIONS

Before starting any construction project, it is important that the engineering properties and characteristics of the soils is investigated. Both field and laboratory investigations required to obtain the necessary data for the soils for this purpose are collectively called soil exploration. The engineering properties of the foundation soil is extremely critical, as choice of the foundation, the bearing capacity, settlement analysis and many important aspects in the design process depends upon the properties of soil.

The term 'Site investigation' refers to the procedure of determining surface and subsurface conditions in the area of proposed construction. It is broader than the scope of 'soil exploration' and includes the latter. Before soil exploration, reconnaissance, study of maps and aerial photography are usually conducted in site investigation. Thus, the process involves complete data collection about a site, and soil exploration is a major part of the investigation.

5.4.1 Preliminary Steps

Preliminary steps are conducted before soil exploration, but they are not mandatory. The objective is to collect the topographical, surface and subsurface conditions before doing the exploration. They help in planning the exploration in an efficient way.

Reconnaissance involves an inspection of the site and an overall study of the topographical features. This will provide information about the soil and ground-water conditions and also help the engineer plan the programme of exploration. Information on surface and subsurface conditions of an area is frequently available in the form of maps. Many authorities in India like the Survey of India and Geological Survey of India, provide topographical maps. Freely available remote sensing data, including satellite sources can also be used. The portal of Geological Survey of India (Bhukosh), National Remote Sensing Centre (Bhuvan), and the US Geological Society are some options where data is available online. Aerial photography is now gaining wide popularity and is helpful for site investigation for any major project. They can be used for multiple applications including the development of topographical maps for the study area.

5.4.2 Soil Exploration

Soil exploration may be needed during new construction, but also when remedial measures are required for any structure due to geotechnical problems. The exploration is generally carried out to achieve the following objectives:

(i) To determine of the nature of the soil deposits
(ii) To determine the location and fluctuations of groundwater
(iii) To determine of the depth and thickness and extent of the soil strata
(iv) To determine the in-situ subsurface properties by performing field tests
(v) To collect soil and rock samples from the various strata for laboratory experiments
(vi) To determine the engineering properties of the soil and rock strata

In general, the methods available for soil exploration may be classified as follows:

5.4.2.1 *Direct Methods*

- **Test pits, trial pits or trenches**

  Test pits or trenches are accessible or open type exploratory methods. In this method, soil can be inspected in their natural condition. The necessary soils samples may be obtained by sampling techniques and can be used for laboratory testing. Test pits will also be useful for conducting field tests such as the plate-load test. Test pits are considered suitable only for small depths. For greater depths, they need to be supported with lateral supports or bracing.

5.4.2.2 *Semi-Direct Methods*

- **Borings**

  Making or drilling bore holes into the ground to collect soil or rock samples from specified depths is called 'boring'. The common methods of advancing bore holes are:

  1. Wash boring
  2. Rotary drilling
  3. Auger boring
  4. Auger and shell boring
  5. Percussion drilling

5.4.2.3 *Indirect Methods*

- **Soundings, penetration tests and geophysical methods**

  These are done with the supply or electricity or with seismic waves. The soil layers are distinguished by observing changes in the electrical resistivity, velocity of waves or in its magnetic and electrical field. Some of the geophysical methods commonly used are electrical resistivity tomography (ERT), crosshole testing, ground penetrating radar (GPR), seismic refraction and reflection, downhole testing, spectral analysis of surface waves (SASW), electromagnetic wave measurement and induced polarization. Soil samples from field cannot be collected with indirect methods and hence they do not give information about the engineering properties of the soil. They are often used in along with direct methods.

5.4.2.4 *Planning an Exploration Programme*

Planning of locations and depths of boring and sampling is the first step of any exploration programme. The two important aspects of a boring programme are 'spacing of borings' and 'depth of borings'.

The number of borings or the spacing of borings for a project depends upon the type, size, and weight of the proposed structure, subsurface conditions, budget, and the local building code guidelines. Before the investigation, a preliminary estimate of the spacing is made. It is modified after reconnaissance and study of other maps, depending upon the local site requirements. The spacings mentioned in Table 5. 5 are recommended in planning an exploration programme. When the subsurface strata have uniform conditions the spacing can be increased to double of these values, and when the conditions are irregular, these should be reduced to the half values.

Table 5.5: Spacing of Borings (Sowers and Sowers, 1970)

Nature of the Project	Spacing of Borings (m)
Highway (subgrade survey)	300 to 600
Borrow pits	30 to 120
Earth dam	30 to 60
Single story factories	30 to 90
Multistorey buildings	15 to 30

To get adequate information for bearing capacity and settlement calculations, the borings should penetrate all strata that get affected by the load of the structure. That is, for important and heavy structures the borings should extend to the bed rock. For smaller structures, shallow borings or the results of investigations from nearby sites can also be used. Table 5. 6 lists the depth of explorations recommended by IS 1892 – 1979 for different construction projects.

Table 5.6: Depth of exploration (IS: 1892-1979)

Nature of the Project	Depth of Exploration (m)
Isolated spread footings or raft or adjacent footings with clear spacing equal or greater than four times the width	One and half times the width
Adjacent footings with clear spacing less than twice the width	One and half times the length
Adjacent rows of footings (i) With clear spacing between rows less than twice the width (ii) With clear spacing between the rows greater than twice the width (iii) With clear spacing between rows greater than or equal to four times the width	 (i) Four and half times the width (ii) Three times the width (iii) One and half times the width
Pile and Well foundations	One and half times the width of structure from bearing level (toe of pile or bottom of well)
Road cuts	Equal to the bottom width of the cut
Fill	Two metres below the ground level or equal to the height of the fill whichever is greater

5.4.3 Field Identification of Soils

Basically, coarse-grained and fine-grained soils are distinguished based on whether the individual soil grains can be seen with naked eye or not. Thus, grain-size itself may be adequate to distinguish between gravel and sand: but silt and clay cannot be distinguished by this technique. Field identification of soils becomes easier if one understands how to distinguish gravel from sand, sand from silt, and silt from clay. While gravel from sand can be distinguished by visual inspection, other classifications require some field tests, which are easy to perform at the field.

5.4.3.1 *Dispersion Test*

This test can be used to distinguish sand from silt and silt from clay. The test consists of pouring a spoonful of sample in a jar of water. Sand settles down in a one or two minutes, but, and silt, may take 15 mins to one hour to settle. Both sand and silt will not be left in the suspension ultimately. If the sample is clay, it will form a suspension which will remain as such for hours, and even for days, provided flocculation does not take place.

5.4.3.2 *Dilatancy Test*

This test is used to distinguish between silt and clay. In this test, a part of the material is placed in one's palm and is shaken. If it is silt, water comes to the surface with a shining appearance. If it is kneaded, the moisture will re-enter the soil and the shine disappear. If it is clay, the water cannot infiltrate easily and hence sample will look dark. If it is a mixture of silt and clay, the relative speed with which the shine appears may give an indication of the amount of silt present. This test is also known as 'shaking test'.

5.4.3.3 *Dry Strength Test*

This test is used to distinguish between silt and clay. A small briquette of material should be dried and tried to be broken. If the briquette can be broken easily, the material is silt. Clay requires more effort to be broken. If the dried briquette has dust particles which can be easily removed, the material is silt. With water, clay gives a soapy touch; it also dries slowly, sticks, and cannot be dusted off easily.

5.4.3.4 *Toughness Test*

This test is also used to distinguish between silt and clay and is similar to the plastic limit test. A thread is attempted to be made with a moist soil sample to a diameter of about 3 mm. It is not possible to make such a thread with silt without crumbling. If it is clay, such a thread can be made even to a length of about 30 cm and supported by its own weight when held at the ends. This is also called the 'rolling test'.

UNIT SUMMARY

This unit discussed one of the important methods of ground improvements in the field, compaction. Compaction is a process in which the soil is densified, and the engineering properties are improved. This process is applied before starting the construction process, to improve the bearing capacity and reduce the settlement of soil, upon the application of load. The chapter also discusses the purpose of soil exploration and different methods used for soil exploration in brief.

EXERCISES

Multiple Choice Questions

1. Compaction of soil is aimed at:

   (a) Decreasing the density (b) Increase porosity

   (c) Decreasing void ratio (d) Decreasing shear strength

2. Compaction of soil is measured in terms of:
   (a) Dry Density (b) Specific Gravity
   (c) Compressibility (d) Permeability
3. Optimum moisture content is the moisture content at which:
   (a) Settlement is minimum (b) Permeability is more
   (c) Dry density is maximum (d) Shear strength is less
4. In which of the following soil type does vibration as a compaction principle work best?
   (a) Clay (b) Sand
   (c) Marshy soil (d) Silt

Answers of Multiple Choice Questions			
1. (c)	2. (a)	3. (c)	4. (b)

Numerical

Examples:

1. What is the theoretical maximum dry density of a soil sample having specific gravity 2.65 and water content 18 %?

$$G = 2.65$$
$$w = 18\ \%$$
$$\rho_{d(theoretical)} = \frac{G\rho_w}{1+wG}$$
$$= \frac{2.65\times 1}{1+0.18\times 2.65}$$
$$= 1.79\ g/cm^3$$

2. A cohesive soil gives maximum dry density of 1.8 g/cm^3 at a water content of 17 %, during a proctor test. If the specific gravity of the soil is 2.7, what is the degree of saturation?

$$G = 2.7$$
$$w = 17\ \%$$
$$\rho_d = 17\ g/cm^3$$
$$\rho_d = \frac{G\rho_w}{1+\frac{wG}{s}}$$
$$1.8 = \frac{2.7\times 1}{1+\frac{0.17\times 2.65}{s}}$$
$$1+\frac{0.17\times 2.65}{s} = \frac{2.7\times 1}{1.8}$$
$$\frac{0.4505}{s} = 1.5-1 = 0.5$$

$$S = \frac{0.4505}{0.5}$$

$$= 0.901 = 90.1\ \%$$

Exercises

1. A laboratory compaction test on soil having specific gravity equal to 2.68 gave a maximum dry density of 1.82 g/cc and a water content of 17% per cm. determine degree of saturation, air content and percentage air voids at maximum dry density. What would be theoretical maximum dry density corresponding to zero air voids at OMC.
2. The following are the results of a compaction test: Volume of mould = 1000ml.
Mass of mould = 1000g Sp. Gravity of mold = 2.70
Determine degree of saturation at maximum dry density?

Mass of mould + wet soil	2935	3096	3152	3124	3056
Water content	10	12.2	14.3	16.2	18.5

3. Work out theoretical maximum dry density for a soil sample having specific gravity of 2.72 and OMC = 16%. Also explain the difference in OMC value in case of proctor test and modified proctor test for cohesive soil and granular soil.
4. A cohesive soil yields a maximum dry density of 1.85 gm/cc at an OMC of 16% during a standard proctor test. If the value of G is 2.63, what is the degree of saturation?

Short and Long Answer Type Questions

1. Enlist the differences between compaction and consolidation.
2. Is compaction test significant in the case of sandy soils? Justify your answer.
3. What are the different methods used for surface compaction?
4. An earthen dam is proposed near your place. While compacting the core of the dam, what moisture content will you suggest? We of optimum or dry of optimum? Why?
5. What do you mean by optimum moisture content?
6. Define zero air void line.
7. Explain the objectives of soil exploration.
8. What is stabilization of soil? What are the different methods?
9. What do you mean by dry of optimum or wet of optimum?
10. What are the different stages involved in site investigation? Explain in detail.

PRACTICALS

Name of experiment: Determination of MDD and OMC of the given soil sample by light compaction (IS 2720)

Aim: To determine the MDD and OMC of the given soil sample by light compaction

Apparatus required: Proctor mould having a capacity of 944 cm³, mechanical operated metal rammer of weight of 2.6 kg, drop of 310mm, arrangement to control the height of drop to a free fall, sample extruder, a weighing balance of 15 kg capacity, and a sensitive balance for moisture content determination, mixing and cutting tools, and containers

Theory: Compaction is the process in which soil partials are artificially rearranged and packed together into closer state of contact by mechanical means in order to reduce void ratio, permeability and compressibility and in order to increase the degree of denseness, stability, shear strength and bearing capacity. The compaction characteristics are first determined in a laboratory by various compaction tests. The relationship between water content and dry density obtained from compaction test is used to determine the MDD and OMC of a sample.

Procedure:

1. Take approximately 3 kg from a representative oven-dried sample, in a pan. Thoroughly mix the sample with sufficient water to dampen it.
2. Weigh the mould without base plate and collar, and also measure the internal dimensions. Fix the collar and base plate. Fill the soil in the mould and in 3 layers giving 25 blows per layer with the 2.6 kg rammer falling through a height of 310 mm.
3. Remove the collar, trim off the excess soil to make a level surface.
4. Weigh the wet sample with the mould.
5. Remove the sample from the mould and take a small sample from the centre, for moisture content determination.
6. Continue the process by increasing the moisture content, till a drop or no change in wet weight of sample is observed.

Observations:

Diameter of the mould ________________ cm
Height of the mould ________________ cm
Volume of the mould (Vs) ____________ cc
Weight of empty mould (Wm) ________ gm

Experiment No.	1	2	3	4	5
Weight of cylinder + compacted soil (Wms) g					
Weight of compacted soil ($Ws = Wms - Wm$) g					
Bulk density of compacted soil ($\rho = \frac{Ws}{Vs}$) g/cm³					
Container No.					
Mass of empty container with lid (wl) g					

Experiment No.	1	2	3	4	5
Mass of container with lid and wet soil ($w2$) g					
Mass of container with lid and dry soil ($w3$) g					
Mass of water ($ww = w2 - w3$) g					
Water content in % $w = (ww / ws) x100$ Dry density of the soil ($\rho_d = \frac{\rho}{1+w}$) g/cm3					

Result:

Inference:

KNOW MORE

Changi East Reclamation projects in Singapore is a good case study for massive ground improvement used for mega projects. Limited land space often demands large reclamations projects for diverse uses. The ground investigation included a significant amount of in-situ testing using a variety of techniques as well as the collection and testing of undisturbed soil samples. Field and laboratory tests were used to obtain the necessary geotechnical parameters for design purposes and decision making for acceptance of ground improvement works. Geotechnical and geotextile laboratories were built up on site for characterization and quality control due to the project's nature and speed. In addition to strengthening the underlying soils, it was necessary to densify hydraulically filled granular soils using deep compaction techniques in order to reduce future immediate settlement and boost liquefaction resistance.

REFERENCES AND SUGGESTED READINGS

- Arora,K.R., "Soil Mechanics and Foundation Engineering," Standard Publishers Distributors, Delhi, 2008.
- Gulhati, S. K.; Datta, M." Geotechnical engineering, Tata McGraw-Hill, New Delhi, 2005.
- Sowers G.B. and Sowers G.F."Soil Mechanics and Foundations", Collier Macmillan Company, Toronto, Canada, 1970.

- IS 1892-1979 (Reaffirmed 2002): Code of practice for subsurface investigations for foundations
- IS 2720 (Part VII) – 1980 (Reaffirmed 2011): Methods of test for soils, Part VII Determination of water content-dry density relation using light compaction.
- IS 2720 (Part VIII) – 1983 (Reaffirmed 2006): Methods of test for soils, Part VIII Determination of water content-dry density relation using heavy compaction.
- IS 2720 (Part XVI) – 1987 (Reaffirmed 2016): Methods of test for soils, Part XVI Laboratory determination of CBR

Dynamic QR Code for Further Reading

Dynamic QR Code for Further Reading

APPENDICES

Appendix-A

Suggestive template for practicals

Name of experiment:

Aim:

Apparatus required:

Procedure:

Observations:

Result:

Inference:

Appendix-B

Indicative Evaluation Guidelines for Practicals / Projects / Activities in Group

Viva (15)	Performance (15)	Interaction (10)	Report (10)	Total (50)

REFERENCES FOR FURTHER LEARNING

- Craig, R.F., "Soil Mechanics", Van Nostrand Reihnold Co. Ltd., London, 1978.
- Das, B.M., "Principles of Geotechnical Engineering", PWS-KENT Publishing Co., Boston, 1985.
- Das, B.M., "Principles of Foundation Engineering", Brooks/Cole Engineering Division, Monterey, 1984. 31.
- Das, B.M., 'Advanced Soil Mechanics", Mc Graw-Hill Book Co., New York, 1985.
- Das, B.M., "Introduction to Soil Mechanics", Galgotia Publication, New Delhi, 1983.
- Deere, D.U., "Geological consideration", Chapter in Rock mechanics in Engineering Practice, edited by Stagg, M.G. and Zienkiewics, O.C., Wiley, 1968.
- Deere, D.U., and R.P. Miller, "Engineering Classification and Index Properties for Intact Rock", Tech. Rep. No. AFWL-TR 65-116, Air Force Weapons Lab., Kirtland Air Base, New Mexico, 1966.
- Hough, B.K., "Basic Soils Engineering", Ronald Press Co., New York, 1969.
- Housel, W.S., "A Practical method for the Selection of Foundation Based on Fundamental Research in Soil Mechanics", Research Bulletin, No. 13, University of Michigan, Ann Arbor, 1929.
- Huntigton, W.C., "Earth Pressure and Retaining Walls", John Wiley & Sons, New York, 1957.
- Hvorslev, M.J., "Subsurface Exploration and Sampling of Soils for Civil Engineering Purposes".
- US. Waterways Experiment Station, Vicksburg, Miss, 1949.
- Jumikis, A.R. "Soil Mechanics", D. Van Nostrand Co., Princeton, NJ, USA, 1962.
- Lambe, T.W. and Whitman, R.V. "Soil Mechanics", John Wiley & Sons, Inc., NY, 1969.
- McCarthy. D.F. "Essentials of Soil Mechanics and Foundations", Reston Publishing Company, Reston, Va, USA, 1977.
- Murthy, V.N.S. Soil Mechanics and Foundation Engineering, Dhanpat Rai and Sons, Delhi-6, 2nd ed., 1977
- Singh A. & Punmia, B.C. "Soil Mechanics and Foundations", Standard Book House, Delhi-6, 1970.

CO AND PO ATTAINMENT TABLE

Course outcomes (COs) for this course can be mapped with the programme outcomes (POs) after the completion of the course and a correlation can be made for the attainment of POs to analyze the gap. After proper analysis of the gap in the attainment of POs necessary measures can be taken to overcome the gaps.

Table for CO and PO attainment

Course Outcomes	ATTAINMENT OF PROGRAMME OUTCOMES (1- Weak Correlation; 2- Medium Correlation; 3- Strong Correlation)						
	PO-1	PO-2	PO-3	PO-4	PO-5	PO-6	PO-7
CO-1							
CO-2							
CO-3							
CO-4							
CO-5							

The data filled in the above table can be used for gap analysis.

INDEX

Active earth pressure 75
Activity of clays 22
Air content 15
Bearing capacity 64
Boring 95
California bearing ratio (CBR) 92
Coefficient of permeability 42
Cohesion 88
Consolidation 90
Compaction 84
Compaction curve 85
Consistency index 21
Consistency limits 20
Constant head permeameter 43
Core-cutter method 17
Darcy's law 41
Degree of saturation 15
Dilatancy test 97
Direct shear test 53
Dispersion test 97
Dry strength test 97
Earth pressure at rest 73
Effective stress 48
Falling head permeameter 43
Flow index 22
Flownet 46
General shear failure 66
Grain size (particle-size) distribution 19
Internal friction 51
Liquid limit 20
Liquidity index 21
Local shear failure 66
Maximum dry density 89
Modified Proctor test 84
Plate load test 69
Pore water pressure 48
Porosity 15
Poorly graded soil 19
Punching shear failure 67
Rammers 90
Rankine's theory 75
Retaining walls 9
Rocks 3
Igneous 4
Sedimentary 6
Metamorphic 6
Rollers 89
Sand-replacement method 17
Seepage pressure 48
Sensitivity of clays 22
Settlement 65
Shallow foundation 64
Shrinkage 21
Index 21
Limit 20
Site investigation 94
Soil exploration 94
Soil stabilisation 90
Specific gravity 17
Standard Penetration test 71
Standard Proctor test 84
Thixotropy 22
Toughness index 22
Toughness test 97
Unconfined compression strength 53
Unit weight 16
Bulk (mass) 16
Dry 16

Mohr-coulomb theory 52
Optimum moisture content 86
Passive earth pressure 75
Percent air voids 15
Permeability 41
Phase diagram 14
Piping 50
Plastic limit 21
Plasticity index 21
Saturated 16
Submerged (buoyant) 16
Soil solids 17
Vane shear test 53
Vibrators 90
Void ratio 15
Water (moisture) content 84
Well-graded soil 19
Zero-air void line 86